EDITOR: MARTIN

OSPREY
MILITARY

MEN-AT-ARM

BRUNSWICK 1809-15

Text by
OTTO VON PIVKA
Colour plates by
BRYAN FOSTEN

Published in 1985 by
Osprey Publishing Ltd
59 Grosvenor Street, London W1X 9DA
© Copyright 1985 Osprey Publishing Ltd
Reprinted 1987, 1989, 1991

British Library Cataloguing in Publication Data

Otto von Pivka
    Brunswick troops, 1809–1815.—(Men-at-arms
    series; 167)
    1. Brunswick (Germany)—Armed Forces
    2. Germany—History, Military—19th century
    I. Title   II. Series
    355′.00943′59   UA718.B7

    ISBN 0-85045-613-4

Filmset in Great Britain
Printed in Hong Kong

Acknowledgements
I wish to acknowledge the invaluable assistance given
to me in the preparation of this book by the
authorities and staff of the Landesmuseum in
Brunswick, the members of the Berlin section of the
Gesellschaft für Heereskunde, my many friends and
comrades in that city, and Philip Haythornthwaite.

Artist's Note
Readers may care to note that the original paintings
from which the colour plates in this book were
prepared are available for private sale. All
reproduction copyright whatsoever is retained by the
publisher. All enquiries should be addressed to:
    Bryan Fosten
    13 The Green
    Hackbridge
    Wallington, Surrey SM6 7AU
The publishers regret that they can enter into no
correspondence upon this matter.

Introduction

Before delving into the details of the uniforms, campaigns and organisation of the troops of the Duchy of Braunschweig-Luneburg-Oels it is necessary to cast a brief look at the political situation in Europe during the Napoleonic era, in order to see why it was that these Germans, with no direct connection to the British crown, entered British service and fought so bravely against Napoleon.

Prior to 1870 Germany, as a cohesive state, did not exist. The area now occupied by the two Germanies (the Federal Republic of Germany in the West and the German Democratic Republic in the East) and by part of what is nowadays Poland, was a rag-tag collection of electorates, duchies, grand duchies, principalities and kingdoms. These states, mostly small, were politically divided among themselves; mutually fearful, and sometimes openly hostile; and, for the most part, without any influence on affairs outside their own very limited borders.

Together with Austria they formed the 'Holy Roman Empire', and some of the rulers had the right to cast a vote in the election of the Emperor[1]. Traditionally, the Emperor was the Austrian head of state but there had been exceptions to this (e.g.

1742–1745, when the Elector Karl Albrecht of Bavaria had occupied the Imperial throne because the Austrian head of state was then a woman, the Queen Maria Theresia.

(Maria Theresia's father had been Emperor Karl VI of the Holy Roman Empire; to ensure the transition of the title to his heir when he died he persuaded most European powers to agree to the Pragmatic Sanction. Bavaria refused to recognise this; on Karl VI's death, Karl Albrecht, Elector of Bavaria, proclaimed himself heir to the Habsburg lands (he was son-in-law of Emperor Joseph I), and with French aid captured Prague in 1741. He then

Karl Wilhelm Ferdinand, Duke of Braunschweig-Oels, and father of the 'Black Duke'; he was mortally wounded at Jena/Auerstadt in October 1806 while serving as a field marshal in the Prussian Army.

[1] At the beginning of the Holy Roman Empire, power was concentrated almost entirely in the hands of the Emperor. Gradually the lesser rulers of the Empire became dissatisfied with this state of affairs, and subsequently an electoral college for the position of Emperor was established. Initially there were seven states whose rulers were also Electors; three were secular—Saxony, Bohemia and Brandenburg; and four were ecclesiastical—the Prince-Bishoprics of Cologne, Trier, Münster and Mainz. The rulers of these states assumed the title 'Elector' (German: Kur) in addition to their existing titles. At the death of the Holy Roman Emperor the electoral college would meet and elect the new Emperor.

In 1648 the electoral college membership was extended to the Palatinate (Pfalz), and in 1692 Brunswick-Luneburg (otherwise Hanover) was added. In 1803 Trier and Cologne were dissolved and four new Electorates were created: Baden, Württemberg, Salzburg and Hessen-Kassel. That same year Hanover was overrun by France and given to Prussia.

Hussar trooper of the 'Black Band' in 1809, wearing the off-white caped greatcoat thrown over his shoulders. Uniform details are given in the body of the text; and cf. the trumpeter, Plate A1. (Beyer-Pegau)

(Centre)
Two Hussar officers, 1809; yellow and silver sabre knots and sashes; gilt chin scales and picker fittings on the pouch belt; and facings and saddle furniture edging in light blue. (Beyer-Pegau)

(Right)
Officer and trumpeter of Hussars, 1809. Note the so-called Polish harness on the officer's charger, with black fringing. See Plates A1, A2. (Beyer-Pegau)

styled himself 'King of Bavaria', and in 1742 had himself elected Holy Roman Emperor. Eventually, in 1744, Maria Theresia forced him to evacuate not only her lands but also his own Bavaria. He died in Munich on 20 January 1745.)

Apart from voting for the Emperor, each state was required to provide a 'Kontingent' of troops when needed by the Emperor for use against the foes of the Empire. This delightfully democratic Imperial military system had obvious disadvantages, however—particularly when one considers all the various and different drill regulations which were used, and the fact that practically every state produced its own firearms, each to its own calibre and specifications.

In short, the Holy Roman Empire as it existed in 1796, when Napoleon burst on to the European military and political scene in a blaze of energy was a colourful but totally outmoded and semi-fossilised institution. For instance, when composing the order

of battle for the polyglot contingents of the Holy Roman Empire, it was customary for the troops belonging to the most senior member of the Imperial hierarchy to form on the right of the line. The other units ranged to its left in order of seniority of their proprietors. Should any unit's proprietor be promoted, or fall from favour, its position in the line of battle immediately had to be altered.

Until 1800 the Imperial forces managed to stay on the battlefield against the revolutionary French forces; but constant bickering among their commanders and their old-fashioned system of tactics ensured that their days were numbered. Finally, at the battle of Hohenlinden in Bavaria on 3 December 1800, the military power of the Holy Roman Empire was shattered, leaving only the gaudy titles—and these too were to vanish in 1805.

In that year Napoleon, now firmly in popular dictatorial command of the French nation and army, was about to extend his grip on the mainland of Europe. This was the era of the Coalition Wars, in which Revolutionary France was opposed by a rapidly changing kaleidoscope of European monarchies whom she repeatedly defeated, or who defeated themselves by dissolving into mutually isolated, hostile, self-seeking sub-groups. Prussia and Austria squabbled over Silesia; Saxony feared annexation by Prussia; Prussia looked nervously towards Russia across her newly acquired Polish provinces; and Britain, although the greatest naval power in the world at that time, did not possess a

4

Items attributed to the Brunswickers of 1809 in the Wehrhistorisches Museum, Rastatt, Baden-Württemberg. They are identified as an officer's sabretasche with silver emblems; a silver death's-head shako plate; a silver star-shaped officer's pouch badge; and an infantry officer's silver and yellow silk sash. The use of the 'W' cypher, as opposed to 'FW', is unexplained, and there appears to be no other source from 1809 with which to compare it. Note narrow dimensions of sash.

large enough army to enter the lists on the European mainland while maintaining her colonial possessions against French and Dutch opposition.

Added to this martial weakness on land was the fact that Napoleon already controlled most of the European coastline facing England, and any attempt at intervention on the continent would thus have opened with an opposed landing on a hostile coast—a task for which the British government and army had little enthusiasm.

Britain's contribution to these early Coalition Wars against France in Europe was mainly limited to two fields: money, and intelligence. British gold paid for the muskets and ammunition of Austrian, Prussian and Russian soldiers while British agents intrigued against France and sought to stiffen their wavering allies.

In 1803 Napoleon had overrun the Electorate of Hanover, thus deepening the rift between France and Britain, whose monarch (George III) was also the Elector of Hanover. Most of the Hanoverian army made its way to England where it became the 'King's German Legion'—see MAA 119, *Wellington's Infantry (2)*. The restless French Emperor was again opposed by yet another unsteady alliance, the 'Third Coalition'. This time Austria and Russia entered the lists against him, backed by British gold and hoping that Prussia and Saxony would aid them in a more direct way. King Frederick William III of Prussia, a weak and vacillating monarch, dithered on the sidelines until it was too late to achieve anything, and thus contributed largely to the Austro-Russian defeats in this campaign.

On 17 October 1805 the Austrian commander in Germany, Feldmarschall-Leutnant Mack, was surrounded and forced to capitulate at Ulm with 20,000 men. Mack had pushed deep into hostile Bavarian territory at the start of this campaign, and was waiting at Ulm to be joined by a strong Russian force when Napoleon, moving with characteristic speed and outnumbering Mack's immediate command by three to one, encircled him and forced a humiliating surrender. The majority of Napoleon's forward troops in this operation were Germans—Bavarians, Württembergers and Badenese; and he was aided in this victory by some incredibly bad

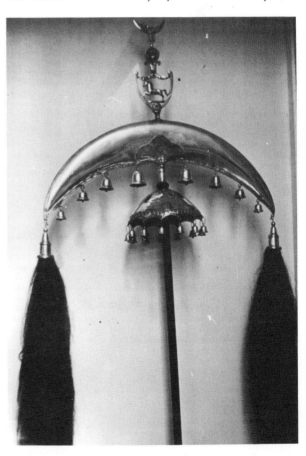

The 1st Battalion of the Brunswick infantry regiment had a band, and in 1809 Queen Charlotte Sophia of England presented it with this *Schellenbaum* or 'Jingling Johnnie'. A unique feature is the downwards sweep of the horns. The *Schellenbaum* was carried by the 92nd (Brunswick) Infantry Regiment of the Imperial German Army until 1918, when it was presented to the Brunswick Landesmuseum. The horse tails were originally red.

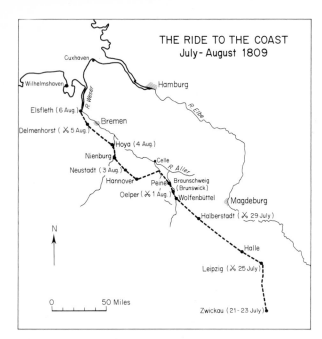

THE RIDE TO THE COAST
July - August 1809

Cuxhaven
Wilhelmshaven
Hamburg
Elsfleth (6 Aug.)
R. Weser
Bremen
Delmenhorst (✗ 5 Aug.)
R. Elbe
Hoya (4 Aug.)
Nienburg
Celle
R. Aller
Neustadt (3 Aug.)
Hannover
Peine
Braunschweig
(Brunswick)
Oelper (✗ 1 Aug.)
Wolfenbüttel
Magdeburg
Halberstadt (✗ 29 July)
N
Halle
Leipzig (✗ 25 July)
0   50 Miles
Zwickau (21 - 23 July)

Map showing the Brunswickers' fighting retreat to the sea, and the waiting Royal Navy flotilla, in 1809.

liaison work by his Austrian and Russian foes[1]. The Russians and Austrians were not yet in the mood to surrender, however; and it needed another crushing defeat, that of Austerlitz on 2 December 1805, to force them to come to terms.

In the subsequent Treaty of Pressburg on 26 December 1805 the Holy Roman Empire was officially dissolved and Emperor Franz II, having already renounced his electoral title, became simply Emperor Franz I of Austria. Titles were not the only things which the Austrian monarch lost, however; the Tyrol and the Inn provinces were given to Bavaria, and Vorarlberg to Württemberg. Both these states then became kingdoms and Baden, also increased in area at Austria's expense, became a grand duchy.

As a lesson to Prussia for her side-line dithering, Napoleon took from her the principalities of Cleve and Neuchatel. Cleve he united with the former Bavarian Duchy of Berg to make the Duchy of Cleve-Berg, which he granted to Murat, his flamboyant cavalry commander. Neuchatel went to Berthier, his chief of staff. In compensation for these territorial losses, Prussia was given Hanover.

[1]At this time the Austrians, like most of their European contemporaries, were using the Gregorian calendar while the Russians were working on the Julian calendar. There was a 12 days' difference between the two. Thus, when Mack was expecting Russian forces to Appear at Ulm on day X, the Russians were not intending to be there until day X plus 12!

This state of affairs was not to last, however. By 1806 Napoleon, seeking a way to come to an agreement with Britain over seaborne trade with Europe, was offering Hanover back to George III, without bothering too much about the protests raised by the Prussian king! Frederick III of Prussia was incensed at being so handled and, in a rare moment of decision, declared war on France. Saxony and Brunswick joined Prussia, and both sides marshalled their forces. Inevitably, Austria and Russia could not be brought to concert their efforts with Prussia, thus presenting Napoleon with yet another splendid opportunity to defeat his enemies in detail.

Gathering his German 'allies' up as he advanced, Napoleon rushed through southern Germany with a force made up of troops of the following states: France, Baden, Württemberg, Bavaria, Frankfurt, Hessen-Darmstadt and Würzburg. He caught the Prussian-Saxon-Brunswick army unprepared, and smashed them at the twin battles of Jena and Auerstädt on 14 October 1806. The then-duke of Brunswick, Duke Karl Wilhelm Ferdinand, a field marshal in the Prussian army, was mortally wounded in this engagement.

As a result of this 'French' victory, Saxony was forced to break her alliance with Prussia and to join the French-controlled Confederation of the Rhine. The Prussian army disintegrated, the remnants fleeing eastwards.

By now Russia had decided to join Prussia in defying Napoleon, but their joint armies were defeated in their turn at Friedland on 14 June 1807. The subsequent Treaty of Tilsit (7 July 1807), signed on a raft moored in the middle of the River Niemen, gave Napoleon yet another opportunity to demonstrate his skill as an inventive European cartographer.

Brunswick was dissolved as a state, its former territories being incorporated into the new Napoleonic kingdom of 'Westfalia', which also included parts of the old states of Hanover and Hessen-Kassel. Prussia lost much land, which went to set up the 'Grand Duchy of Warsaw'; and Saxony also gained some territory at Prussia's expense, and was elevated from an electorate to a kingdom, joining the Confederation of the Rhine at the same time. The king of Saxony was also created grand duke of Warsaw, but as Warsaw was an independent member of the Confederation of the Rhine the

Infantry pattern shako, 1809: the death's-head is silver, the chin scales in this case are brass. Some sources show officers wearing silver chin scales; others, plain black straps. This must presumably be either a hussar's or an infantry officer's headgear; a good deal of variation in such details is not uncharacteristic of the period. (Landesmuseum Braunschweig)

Saxon king's secondary title was somewhat hollow.

Europe lapsed once more into an uneasy peace. It is against this violent and turbulent background that we begin our detailed study of the 'Black Brunswickers'.

1809: 'The Black Band'

When the Duchy of Brunswick was dissolved in 1807 the son of the dead duke, the now-dispossessed Friedrich Wilhelm, fled to Austrian territory to nurture in exile his hatred of the French dictator.

Until 1808 peace again reigned on the European mainland; but in that year war broke out in the Spanish peninsula when the proud Spaniards rejected the new king, Joseph Bonaparte—Napoleon's brother—whom the Corsican had attempted to force down their throats.

Since the bitter defeats and loss of territory of 1805, Austria had been hard at work overhauling and expanding her military machine. Although much had been accomplished in this field, Archduke Charles, brother of Emperor Franz I and

the man in overall charge of these army reforms, was not convinced that the Austrian forces were yet in a state to be matched against the French army. His protests were overridden, however, as the Austrian government felt that with the outbreak of the Spanish war Napoleon would have too much to do to be able to devote large forces to deal with them.

Apart from the regular Austrian forces, extensive Landwehr (militia) formations had been raised, equipped, armed and semi-trained; and a number of volunteer corps were also raised. On 25 February 1809 Friedrich Wilhelm of Brunswick entered into an agreement with the Austrians to raise a corps of infantry and cavalry to fight alongside them as they invaded his old domains, raising the population against their French rulers.

Initially this corps was to consist of an infantry regiment and a hussar regiment each of 1,000 men. The infantry regiment was organised in two battalions each of four companies, and the hussar regiment had eight squadrons. The hussar regiment had an attached horse artillery battery consisting of two 7-pdr. howitzers and two 6-pdr. cannon.

To set the new corps on its feet the Austrian government provided 1,000 each of the following items: infantry shakos, hussar shakos, pairs of shoes, pairs of hussar boots (Czismen), pairs of spurs, hussar-pattern waistbelts, cavalry cartridge pouches, infantry cartridge pouches, infantry overcoats, sets of hussar-pattern harness, carbines, infantry muskets with slings, brace of pistols; the cloth ('pepper-and-salt' mixture) for 1,000 cavalry greatcoats; two light 7-pdr. howitzers and two light 6-pdr. cannon, with all accessories; eight ammunition wagons, and 240 rounds for each gun, together with the necessary case shot cartridges; 240 rounds of ammunition per head for each infantryman and cavalryman; 12,000 musket and 12,000 pistol flints; and 25 Windbüchsen. This last was a repeating air rifle, invented by Girardoni, capable of firing 12 rounds at an effective range of about 200 paces, almost noiselessly, before requiring a recharged air cylinder. For its era it was a very advanced weapon but it required skilful maintenance and after Girardoni's death it fell into disuse.

The town of Nachod in Bohemia was designated as the forming-up place for the Brunswick corps, and on 1 April 1809 both the infantry and cavalry

Horse artillery gunner, 1809. He wears the infantry shako; a short *Kollet* jacket with six rows of black lace on the chest and three rows of spherical black buttons; light blue collar, Polish cuffs, shoulder straps, and overall piping. Leather is black with brass fittings, and the brass-hilted sabre has a steel scabbard. Officers wore infantry shakos and *Polrock* coats, with legwear, sashes, and equipment as for Hussar officers, and a heart-shaped gilt shield on the pouch belt bearing the 'FW' cypher. (Beyer-Pegau)

(*Right*) Officer and trooper of the Hussar Regiment in British service in Spain—cf. Plate C. (Beyer-Pegau)

regiments assembled for the first time.

The dispossessed Friedrich Wilhelm of Brunswick was obsessed with the idea of revenge against Napoleon for the damage which had been done to his family and lands. As a physical expression of this vengeance he decided to clothe his new troops all in black, and adopted as his badge the skull-and-crossbones. He thus became known as *Der Schwarzer Herzog* ('the Black Duke'), and his corps was christened *Die Schwarze Schar* ('the Black Band').

The campaign of 1809

Austria judged the time right to strike at the French despite the warning of Archduke Charles to the War Council that the Landwehr was not yet ready for general combat.

By the terms of the Treaty of Pressburg (26 December 1805) Austria had lost the Tyrol to Bavaria. She now fomented discontent among the Tyroleans, who were to rise against the Bavarian occupation forces and eject them from their mountain province. Apart from the Tyrol, Austria had lost many Italian, Illyrian and Dalmatian territories and was ringed with foes. Russia was not in any fit state to undertake operations on Austria's side; and Prussia, still stunned by the dreadful collapse of her army in 1806, was most unco-operative and almost hostile towards Austria. Britain provided plenty of financial aid, but her only armed intervention was in Portugal.

The rest of the German states were now safely welded to the side of France in the Confederation of the Rhine, and even if they secretly wished to help Austria they were quite unable to make any overt moves.

Napoleon, well informed of Austria's military preparations, ordered her to disarm; but in April 1809 Austria opened hostilities at four points. Archduke Ferdinand d'Este was ordered to invade Poland. He initially met with easy success, and entered Warsaw with 36,000 men. He was opposed by a 14,000-strong Saxon-Polish force under Prince Poniatowski; the main armies of Saxony and Poland were employed in Austria and Spain.

After the battle of Raszyn on 19 April 1809, the

Saxon contingent of Poniatowski's force ($2\frac{1}{2}$ battalions of infantry) were recalled to Saxony. In Saxony itself, Oberst Thielmann had been placed in command of a force put together from various depot troops which later grew to eight battalions of infantry each of 1,000 men, and half a battalion of the Leib-grenadiergarde. These troops opposed the Austrian force under Generalmajor am Ende which was in and around Theresienstadt in Bohemia. Part of this force was made up of the Black Band of the Duke of Brunswick and the Kurhessischen Korps of the deposed Prince of Hessen-Kassel. The Austrian forces in Bohemia remained on the defensive, and did not invade Saxony until after a certain amount of provocation on the part of the Saxons under Oberst Thielmann. Encouraged by the inaction of his opponents, Thielmann invaded Bohemia on 25 May 1809, while on 30 and 31 May 1809 the Black Band of the Duke of Brunswick stormed and captured the Saxon town of Zittau. Thielmann then withdrew to Dresden.

After the battle of Aspern Esslingen (21/22 May 1809) Archduke Charles of Austria reinforced General am Ende's force to 10,000 men (Line, Landwehr, Brunswickers and Hessians) and ordered him to make a diversionary raid into Saxony.

A contemporary plate by the brothers Cornel and Christian Suhr showing Allied troops in Hamburg, 1813–15; in this case, three Brunswickers, a Hanseatic Legion infantry officer, and an officer of the Prussian 1st Leib-Husaren. (*Left*) Infantry officer, in *Polrock* or *Litewka* with silver sash, and picker equipment. The silver cuff facing edging is of interest. The only false note is the apparently Prussian black and silver cockade on the shako. Facings, and overall stripes, are light blue. (*2nd left*) Hussar officer in undress cap, and pelisse worn as jacket. Note bag-shaped cap crown with silver tassel, and small death's-head badge on light blue band. (*Centre*) Hussar officer in dolman and shako; this seems to differ from written sources in several details. Again, a Prussian shako cockade is worn; there is no gold top band, and a cord of some kind is shown here. The light blue collar and cuffs of the dolman have silver, rather than black lace decoration.

Sergeant-major of 1st Line Infantry Bn., 1815—cf. Plate F3 for comparison of NCO features. Collar, shoulder straps and trouser piping are red; plume, light blue over yellow; cap plate and chevrons, silver. The narrow waist sash and the sabre knot are yellow and light blue; the NCO's plain belly-pouch is shown, partly hidden by the tankard; and note cane of office, hooked to the top left jacket button and thrust through the sabre cross belt. This supports sabre and bayonet scabbards. Note white gloves. (Beyer-Pegau)

Officer's shako, 1st Light Bn., 1815; the top band is of black velvet. (Landesmuseum Braunschweig)

Westfalia) Jerome was very slow to concentrate his forces and come to the aid of the Saxon king.

On 24 June Jerome's force consisted of:

X Corps of the 1st German Army
1st Westfalian Guards Division
Commander: Divisionsgeneral Graf Bernterode

One squadron Garde du Corps	...140 men
One battalion Grenadiergarde	...840 men
One battalion Jägergarde	...600 men
Three squadrons Chevaulegersgarde	...550 men
One battalion Jäger-Carabiniers	...360 men
Total:	2,490 men

2nd Westfalian Division
Commander: Divisionsgeneral D'Albignac

1st Westfalian Line Infantry Regt.	...1,680 men
5th Westfalian Line Infantry Regt.	...1,800 men
6th Westfalian Line Infantry Regt.	...1,700 men
1st Westfalian Kürassier Regt.	...260 men
Total:	5,440 men

3rd Dutch Division
Commander: Divisionsgeneral Gration

6th Dutch Line Infantry Regt.
7th Dutch Line Infantry Regt.
8th Dutch Line Infantry Regt.
9th Dutch Line Infantry Regt.
2nd Dutch Kürassier Regt.
Three companies of artillery

Total: 5,300 men

Also in Westfalia were the following forces:

Commander: Oberst Chabert
3rd Bergisch Line Inf. Regt.—1,000 men in Kassel

28th French Light Inf. Regt.
22nd French Line Inf. Regt.
27th French Line Inf. Regt.
30th French Line Inf. Regt.
33rd French Line Inf. Regt.
65th French Line Inf. Regt.

} 3,000 men in all, partly in Hamburg and partly in Magdeburg.

In addition to these mobile forces, there were 2,300 Mecklenburgers and 800 Oldenburgers as garrisons in the fortresses along the Oder as follows:

Stettin...400 men under Brigadegeneral Liebert
Stralsund...1,100 men under Brigadegeneral Candras
Küstrin...2,000 men (commander unknown)

On 10 June 1809 this raid began, and the Duke of Brunswick moved his corps out of the town of Aussig.

Thielmann, whose forces had brushed with the Brunswickers already, evacuated Dresden and moved all his forces to Gorbitz; and next day, 11 June 1809, the combined forces of General am Ende occupied Dresden. On 12 June the Brunswickers and some Austrian Jägers advanced on Gorbitz and pushed Thielmann and the Saxons back via Pennrich, Wilsdruff and Birkenhain to Nessen; the Saxons lost ten killed and 47 wounded.

The king of Saxony had appealed to King Jerome of Westfalia to come to his aid. This monarch, another of Napoleon's brothers, collected a sizeable force of French, Dutch, Westfalian and Bergisch troops; but due to the activities of the Prussian Major von Schill (who, with his 2nd (Brandenburg) Hussar Regiment, had broken out of his garrison at Potsdam without the approval or knowledge of his king, and was now rampaging his way through the old Prussian provinces of

Thielmann's Saxon corps of about 2,000 men consisted of:

Four squadrons, 'von Zastrow' Kürassiers
One squadron, 'von Polens' Chevaulegers
Three squadrons, Saxon Hussars
Grenadier-Bataillon 'von Einsiedel'
Combined Infantry Battalion 'Welan'
Two companies, Inf. Regt. 'von Burgsdorf'
One musketeer battalion, Infantry Regt. 'von Oebschelwitz'
Two and a half foot artillery batteries
One horse artillery battery

Jerome sent part of his Guards Division and the 3rd Bergisch Infantry Regiment to Eisenach to reinforce the Saxon king's personal guard; and on 18 June 1809 he left Kassel with the rest of the Guards Division, the 2nd Westfalian Division and the 3rd Dutch Division, crossed the River Saale and on 25 June entered Merseburg.

Meanwhile the Austrians and Brunswickers had on 22 June occupied Leipzig (where the Gelernte Jägers were raised); but on the approach of Jerome's superior forces they left the city again on 24 June. Jerome entered the city amid pealing church bells and much public jubilation on 26 June. On 28 June the 2nd Westfalian Division had a brush with the Brunswickers.

The Austrian forces in the area were now formed into the XI Corps under Feldmarschall-Leutnant Freiherr von Kienmayer, and the main weight of their offensive was transferred south into Franconia. By dint of skilful use of mobility, the Austrian-Brunswick forces avoided battle with their enemies and kept them off balance. Leaving a 'bait' of some Landwehr battalions on the road to Dresden, the Austro-Brunswick main force slipped off south. On 1 July 1809 Jerome entered Dresden, but his foes had long since gone. He sent General von Bongars

Officers in undress, 1815—see Plate E1. (*Left*) Subaltern of the Leib-Bataillon, with light blue facings and waistcoat, and dark green gloves. (*Right*) Field officer, 2nd Line Bn., with dark green facings and waistcoat, and silver sleeve decoration. (Beyer-Pegau)

Surviving dolman and waistcoat of a Leib-Bataillon company officer, 1815. Note the narrow shoulders, giving the sleeves a puffed effect at the shoulder seam; the black lace embroidery on the forearms; and the silver lace embroidery and silver ball buttons of the waistcoat. The dolman buttons are covered in black silk; though hidden here, its pale blue collar is embroidered in black. (Landesmuseum Braunschweig; photo courtesy G. A. Embleton)

in pursuit, but Bongars followed a cold trail to Halle in Saxony. Until 4 July Jerome stayed in Dresden; he then moved off south to Hof, where he hoped to join up with Junot's corps which was already in Franconia.

Kienmayer and the Austrians had been pushed out of Nürnberg by Junot with 10,000 men; they fell back towards Hof, and took the offensive against Junot on 8 July at Berneck and Gefraess. Having halted the French, Kienmayer turned on Jerome and confronted him at Hof on 11 July, after having spent two days in Bayreuth.

Jerome, who was at Plauen, then fell back to Schleitz; Kienmayer followed, and confronted him there again on 13 July. After a few cannon shots Jerome fell back to Neustadt an der Orla, where there was another skirmish. On 15 July Jerome fell back again to Erfurt, which he reached on 17 July.

His withdrawal was beginning to resemble a rout, and Jerome's effort to join up with Junot had ended in near-disaster. At Erfurt Jerome heard that an armistice had been signed between France and Austria; and, without waiting to ensure that Saxony no longer required the aid for which she had initially asked, he thankfully hurried back to his capital at Kassel, with 2,000 men of the Guards Division, his Kürassier regiment, the 1st and 6th Westfalian Line Infantry and the 3rd Bergisch Infantry Regiment. Gratien's 3rd Dutch Division remained in Erfurt, and Thielmann's Saxons remained in Saxony. (Napoleon was furious with the X Corps' conduct of the whole campaign.)

The armistice had been signed at Znaim on 12 July 1809, and Kienmayer's Austrians ceased fighting. The Black Duke did not consider himself in any way bound by this armistice, however; in fact, it left him in a hopeless position. He therefore decided to fight his way out to the north German coast, where he hoped to be able to get his force to England on British warships. Most of his corps seemed quite happy at this prospect of a self-imposed exile in a foreign land, but a small number of his officers requested termination of their commissions, and attempted to spread disaffection among the loyal men.

The fight to the coast

The Black Duke parted from the Austrians; and on 26 July (after the 3rd Infantry Battalion had been formed, and the Uhlans had joined the Hussars at Zwickau) he entered Halle in the kingdom of Westfalia, emptied the public chests, recruited new men, and pulled down the Westfalian crest. The next day Jerome ordered General Rewbell in Hanover, General Gratien in Erfurt and General Michaud in Magdeburg, to close in on the duke and destroy him.

Rewbell collected together in Celle the 1st and 6th Westfalian Line Infantry Regiments, the 1st Westfalian Kürassier Regiment, the 3rd Bergisch Line Infantry Regiment and ten guns, and ordered the 5th Westfalian Infantry Regiment to join him: this latter unit was in Halberstadt on 29 July and was 3,000 men strong. The Black Duke heard that they were in an exposed position in the town, and resolved to attack them. At this time, his forces consisted of:

Infantry
Commander: Oberst von Bernewitz
1st Battalion ...500 men under Major von
    Fragstein
2nd Battalion ...500 men under Major von
    Reichmeister
3rd Battalion ...150 men under Major von
    Herzberg
Scharfschützen ...150 men under Major von
    Scriever
Cavalry
Hussars ...550 men under Major Schrader, as
    Oberstlieutenant von Steinmann was recovering
    from a wound.
Uhlans ...80 men under Rittmeister Graf von
    Wedell.
Artillery
Premier-Lieutenant Genderer: 4 guns—80 men
Total: 100 officers and 2,010 men

The 5th Westfalian Infantry Regiment got news
of the approach of the Black Band and set about
putting Halberstadt, an old walled town, into a
good state of defence. At 6 pm on 29 July the
Brunswickers arrived outside the walls and the
Westfalian commanding officer, Oberst Graf
Wellingerode, sent out a few companies of his
regiment to throw them back. A few rounds of
canister from the duke's artillery sent them scuttling
back into the town, and the gates were hurriedly
shut and barred. Surrounding the town with
patrols, the duke assembled assault columns; he led
one of them against the Harsleber Gate while
another column assaulted the Kuhlinger Gate.
Here the fighting was heavy and the casualties
numerous until the gates were shot in by a gun
crewed by officers. The Brunswick Scharfschützen
then rushed in, and pulled away some carts full of
manure which blocked the road behind the gate;
the Brunswickers poured into the town, shouting
'*Sieg oder Tod!*' ('Victory or Death').

At the Harsleber Gate the fight had also cost the
lives of many of the Black Band before a Lieutenant
von Hertell, of the 2nd Infantry Battalion,
succeeded in setting fire to the wooden obstructions
in the gateway. Two companies of the 2nd Battalion
managed to cut down the postern gate of the
Johannis Gate and also gained entrance to the
town.

Interesting dolman or 'Spencer' of a sergeant-major of the
Leib-Btl., which seems to combine officer's and NCO's
features. See Plate G3. (Landesmuseum Braunschweig; photo
courtesy G. A. Embleton)

The cavalry of the Black Band now entered the
town by the Kuhlinger Gate, and rushed through
the streets until they came upon the enemy reserve
of some hundreds of men in the main square. It was
now dark, and the reserve thought that they were
confronted by superior forces: when challenged to
throw down their weapons and surrender, they did
so. During a period of house-to-house fighting the
Westfalian commander was captured by a bold
officer of the Black Hussars, as was the commandant
of the town, Platzmajor Stockmayer; and gradually
the fighting died down. Only some hundreds of
Westfalians held out in a big house near the Breiten
Gate until dawn.

Next day the Brunswickers found that they had
captured 80 officers and 2,000 men, and that the
Westfalian dead and wounded numbered about
600. Among the dead were about 20 of the
Westfalian Gensdarmes, an organisation liberally
hated by the Brunswickers. The flags of the 5th
Westfalian Infantry Regiment were also taken, but

what happened to them is a mystery. About 100 Westfalians escaped. The Brunswickers' losses were 400 men killed and wounded.

After replenishing his ammunition and equipment from captured stocks, and recruiting over 300 men from the Westfalian soldiers, the Black Duke pushed on to his old capital of Brunswick, which he reached on the evening of 31 July.

On 1 August he fought his way through a Westfalian and Bergisch force under General Rewbell at Oelper. There was no uprising in the duke's favour, probably because the hoped-for British invasion of north Germany had not occurred and only a few gunboats had in fact appeared.

After the skirmish at Oelper, Rewbell pulled off north towards Celle and then re-advanced on

Private, 3rd Line Bn., 1815: it is hard to make out if this unconvincing bell-shaped shako is meant to represent the normal tapered style or the Russian-type *kiwer*. The pompon is light blue over yellow, the plate silver, the facings white, the leather equipment black, and the British-style water-bottle light blue. Cf. Plate H1.

Oelper, only to find that the Black Duke had gone towards Hannover; and, on 4 August, further on to Hoya. Rewbell followed slowly via Burgdorf, crossed the River Leine, and continued north-west to Hoya on the Weser. Rewbell had no certain information concerning the duke's movements, and did not seem too keen to catch him—the bridge over the Weser had anyway been destroyed by the duke's men, which further slowed the pursuit. The Black Duke went now to Delmenhorst, but left a weak rearguard behind with instructions to withdraw north towards Bremen and thus to lead the enemy away from his real embarkation point, which was Elsfleth on the west bank of the Weser.

This ruse succeeded, and after a skirmish at Heidkrug the rearguard were able to rejoin the main body at Elsfleth on 6 August, leaving Rewbell slowly marching and countermarching, trying to decide which trail to follow. The Black Band (now 1,600 men strong) even had time to sell off their horses before embarking on English ships, which took them first to Heligoland and thence to the Isle of Wight. There they underwent a period of re-organisation, before entering British service and fighting in the Peninsula.

King Jerome was furious with Rewbell, who had previously been his favourite, and sent General Bongars to Bremen on 10 August with orders removing Rewbell from his command. Rewbell, however, was not to be found: sensing that things might be getting unpleasant, he had slipped aboard ship and was now on his way to America.

The Peninsular War, 1810-14

The Infantry

On 8 October 1810 the 'Brunswick-Oels Jägers'—as the infantry regiment was now known—landed in Lisbon. They apparently comprised 12 companies and a regimental headquarters, and initially went to Pakenham's brigade in Cole's 4th Division. Shortly afterwards they were transferred to General Crauford's Light Division; and as part of this crack formation they took part in the pursuit of Marshal Masséna from the Lines of Torres Vedras on 17 November 1810, and in the skirmish at Santarem

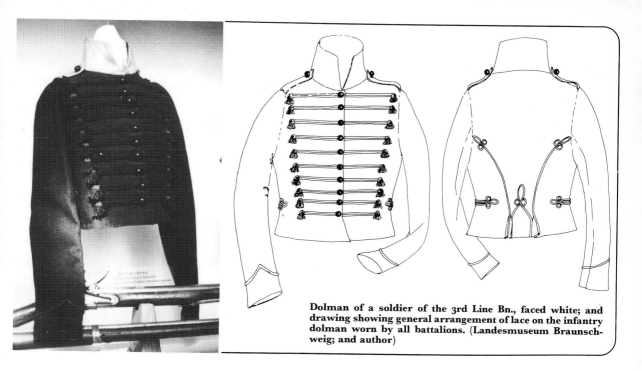

Dolman of a soldier of the 3rd Line Bn., faced white; and drawing showing general arrangement of lace on the infantry dolman worn by all battalions. (Landesmuseum Braunschweig; and author)

on 19 November. Other actions in which they participated with the Light Division were Redinha (12 March 1811); Casal Novo (14 March 1811) and Foz d'Arouce (16 March 1811).

After this they were transferred from the Light Division to the newly formed 7th Division, which they joined before April 1811. They served in Von Alten's brigade with a strength of the regimental HQ and nine companies, the other companies being detached as follows: 4th Division (General Lowry Cole)—one company in Ellis's brigade; 5th Division (General Leith)—one company in Greville's brigade and one company in Pringle's brigade. (The officers commanding the formations mentioned above changed frequently during the war and successive commanders' names can be found in Oman's excellent *History of the Peninsular War*.)

At the battle of Fuentes d'Oñoro on 3–5 May 1811 the main body of the Brunswickers with the 7th Division were in a very exposed position, on a ford over the Don Casas River at a village called Pozo Velho on the right flank of the British position. The 7th Division was an untried polyglot force; the other units in the brigade with the Brunswickers were the 85th Line (British), the 2nd (Portuguese) Caçadores, and the Chasseurs Britanniques (a French emigré unit). The 7th Division was not intended to get seriously involved in the battle, but General Marchand's division of Masséna's army fell upon it and pushed it back on to the main British position. The losses which the Brunswickers suffered are shown in the table below.

After the battle the 7th Division marched into Estramadura and took part in the abortive siege of Badajoz, the Brunswickers suffering casualties in two unsuccessful assaults on the outwork of San Cristobal on the nights of 6 and 9 June 1811. The siege was then lifted due to the approach of a relief force under Soult. The 7th Division had no more combats of note during that year.

In 1812 they were present at the final siege of Badajoz, as were the 4th and 5th Divisions, whose casualties in the storming attempts are shown in the attached table. The 7th Division had no casualties. The Brunswickers were at the battle of Salamanca on 22 July 1812, but were not heavily engaged and had no casualties. At the battle of Vittoria on 21 June 1813 they suffered some losses, and some more at the battles of Maya and Roncevalles on 25 July that same year. The detached company with the 4th Division was again engaged in the first battle of Sorauren on 28 July, and the main body of the regiment lost some men in the second battle of Sorauren on 30 July.

At the skirmish of Echalar on 2 August 1813 the

Losses of the Brunswick-Oels Jägers in the Peninsula

Battle and Date	Parent Formation	Killed: Offrs.	Men	Wounded: Offrs.	Men	Missing: Offrs.	Men	Total
Fuentes d'Oñoro 5 May 1811	7th Div.	-	1	1	6	-	10	18
Siege of Badajoz 9 June 1811	7th Div.	-	1	1	3	-	-	7
Siege of Badajoz 6 April 1812	4th Div. 5th Div.	-	7	2	26	-	-	35
Vittoria 21 June 1813	4th Div. 5th Div. 7th Div.	1	-	-	5	-	-	6
Maya 25 July 1813	7th Div.	-	8	3	15	-	15	41
Roncevalles 25 July 1813	4th Div.	-	2	-	2	-	-	4
1st Sorauren 28 July 1813	4th Div.	-	1	-	3	-	1	5
2nd Sorauren 30 July 1813	7th Div.	-	2	-	1	-	14	17
Skirmish at Echalar 2 August 1813	7th Div.	-	1	4	7	-	2	14
Siege of St Sebastian 31 August 1813	5th Div.	-	2	1	6	1	5	15
Crossing of the Bidassoa 7 Oct. 1813	1st Div. 4th Div.	-	7	7	18	-	-	32
The Nive 9 Dec. 1813	5th Div.	-	2	-	1	-	1	4
10 Dec. 1813	5th Div.	-	-	1	2	-	-	3
11 Dec. 1813	5th Div.	-	1	1	1	-	-	3
Orthez 27 Feb 1814	7th Div.	2	5	5	32	-	4	48
Totals		3	40	26	130	1	52	252

main body was again in action; as were the two detached companies in the 5th Division at the siege and storm of the fortress of St Sebastian on 31 August 1813. By the time of the crossing of the Bidassoa (7 October 1813) a company of the Brunswick-Oels Jägers was with the 1st Division, and both these and their comrades in the 4th Division were engaged that day. The main body of the Jägers (still in the 7th Division) were engaged in the battles of the Nivelle (10 November 1813) and the Nive (9 December 1813). The company in the 5th Division also had losses in this latter battle, and on the next day. (The strength of the main body of the Brunswick-Oels Jägers in the 7th Division at the battle of Nivelle was 42 officers and 457 men.)

The Brunswickers' last battle in the Peninsular campaign was that of Orthez on 27 February 1814, where the Brunswickers in the 7th Division were quite heavily involved.

The Hussars

The cavalry of the Black Band were re-organised into a regiment of hussars which was also sent to Spain, but to the eastern side of the peninsula, where they operated in a force made up largely of foreign levies which was used in amphibious operations along the Spanish coast. This force, commanded by Sir John Murray, included British, Portuguese, Spanish and Italian troops.

The Brunswick Hussars, two squadrons strong, landed at Alicante, direct from England, in July 1813, and then took part in the raid on Tarragona. This raid, initially very successful, was badly managed by a timid commander and developed into a farce, culminating in a disgracefully hurried evacuation of the force back on to its ships in which much valuable equipment, including many cannon, was abandoned. Sir John Murray was later court-martialled.

On 25 August 1813 the Brunswick Hussars, with 18 officers and 258 troopers, were part of Lord Bentinck's brigade in this British force on the east coast of Spain. At the combat of Villa Franca on 13 September 1813 they lost one officer and eight men killed, two officers and 24 men wounded and 18 men missing. In 1814 they took part in the invasion of Sicily.

The 1815 Campaign

The Brunswick-Oels Jägers returned home and left British service on 25 December 1814, but the Hussars remained in British service until mid-1815.

When the Russian and Prussian armies had flooded across north Germany in 1813 the Duke of Brunswick-Oels had been confirmed in his family possessions, and at once set about raising new forces which could be used to speed Napoleon's downfall. The first unit raised was a company of Gelernte Jäger, which was completed on 1 January 1814. By 16 March 1814 a second company had been formed. Before the year was out Brunswick's forces comprised:

Leichte-Infanterie-Brigade:
The Avantgarde The original infantry of the Black Band now returned from English service and gathered in two Light Infantry companies; plus the two new Gelernte Jäger companies.
The Leib-Bataillon A new Leib-Bataillon raised from a cadre of the old Black Band, and initially known as the Leichte-Bataillon von Prostler (the name of its commander); on 14 April 1815 this unit became the Leib-Bataillon.
1st, 2nd and 3rd Leichte-Bataillone Newly raised troops.
Linien-Infanterie-Brigade:
1st, 2nd and 3rd Linien-Infanterie-Bataillone Newly raised troops.
Reserve-Infanterie-Brigade:
1st, 2nd, 3rd, 4th and 5th Reserve-Infanterie-Bataillone and a type of Landwehr.
The Husaren-Regiment:
This included a squadron of Uhlans. All personnel were newly raised troops.
Artillery: (All newly raised troops)
One foot battery—8 guns, 188 men.
One horse artillery battery—8 guns, 227 men.
The military train.

Apart from the hussars listed above, the old hussars of the original Black Band were still in English service.

With the exception of the Reserve-Infanterie-Brigade, these forces were present at Quatre Bras and at Waterloo.

The Hundred Days

Napoleon left his exile island of Elba on 26 February

1815, and landed on 1 March between Frejus and Antibes with a force of about 1,000 men. The European monarchs were still busy in Vienna, hammering out the post-war map of the continent, but Bonaparte's re-appearance galvanised them into action. The French army flocked to rejoin their eagles; Louis XVIII fled to Belgium, and a war-weary Europe took up the sword once again. The armies of Britain, the Netherlands, Prussia, Russia, Austria and their minor allies were mobilised, and divided into six main groups to combat their French adversaries. The northernmost group was a British, Hanoverian, Netherlands, Nassau and Brunswick force of 95,000 men under the Duke of Wellington in Belgium. To the south-east of this army were 124,000 Prussians under Blücher; 200,000 Russians were advancing on the Saar; Prince Schwarzenberg (the allied supreme commander) was at the head of 210,000 Austrians advancing via Basle into southern France; and two smaller armies, composed of Austrians and Sardinians, were crossing the Alps from Italy to invade the southernmost parts of France.

From their various mobilisation points these armies had different distances to cover, and not all of them were in the same state of readiness for active service. It thus transpired that the armies of Wellington and Blücher were in position just over the French border in Belgium, and ready for action, by early June 1815, far in advance of their allies.

Napoleon's intelligence service informed him of the dispositions of his enemies, and he quickly deduced that his northernmost foes, Wellington and Blücher, were by far the most serious threat to his plans. He thus resolved to attack them first, to gain a quick victory (and Brussels, a capital city), and to negotiate with his remaining foes from a position of strength. A potential weakness of the Wellington-Blücher position was that the two army groups had divergent lines of communication: Wellington's lay north-west to the ports of Ostend and Antwerp, and Blücher's lay due east to Prussia. Napoleon hoped to exploit this situation by striking at the junction of the two armies and defeating first one and then the other, thus causing them to withdraw along their lines of communication, losing touch with one another and thus worsening their own positions.

On 15 June 1815 the French army crossed the Belgian border near Charleroi and attacked the western flank of the Prussian army. Wellington and Blücher were taken by surprise, but Blücher reacted in character. From his headquarters in Namur he ordered three of his four corps to concentrate at Sombreffe to give battle to the French.

There followed the battle of Ligny on 16 June, in which the Prussians were defeated, falling back initially along their lines of communication to the east—which was just what Napoleon wanted. In order to ensure that their eastern progress would be maintained, Napoleon sent Marshal Grouchy to follow them up and keep them away from their British-Netherlands allies.

At the same time, Napoleon despatched Marshal Ney north along the Charleroi–Brussels road to seize and hold the crossroads at Quatre Bras—a vital junction for the co-operation of the two allied armies. At Quatre Bras on 16 June Ney was opposed by a force under the Prince of Orange, son of the King of the Netherlands; and it was here that the 'Black Brunswickers' came under fire again.

Quatre Bras, 16 June 1815

The Prince of Orange—a young, rash and inexperienced officer—commanded the First Corps of Wellington's army, and it was troops of this corps which were in possession of the vital crossroads on the evening of 15 June when Ney's advanced guard cavalry arrived to take it. After a short fight, Ney called off the attack until the next day. The Netherlands forces at Quatre Bras on the 15th were Col. Gödecke's 2nd Brigade of De Perponcher's 2nd Dutch-Belgian Division:

> 2nd Nassau Inf. Regt.—3 battalions, 2,709 men
>
> Regt. of Orange Nassau—2 battalions, 1,591 men
>
> Battery of Dutch Horse Artillery—8 guns

Col. Gödecke surrendered command of this brigade to Prince Bernhard of Saxe-Weimar on the evening of 15 June.

Ney's forces at Quatre Bras were General Count Reille's Second Corps:

5th Division (Lt.Gen. Baron Bachelu)

> 2nd Light Inf. Regt. ⎫
> 61st Line Inf. Regt. ⎪
> 72nd Line Inf. Regt. ⎬ 11 battalions
> 108th Line Inf. Regt. ⎭

6th Division (Prince Jerome Napoleon)

1st Light Inf. Regt.	
1st Line Inf. Regt.	
2nd Line Inf. Regt.	11 battalions
3rd Line Inf. Regt.	

9th Division (Lt.Gen. Count Foy)

4th Light Inf. Regt.	
92nd Line Inf. Regt.	
93rd Line Inf. Regt.	10 battalions
100th Line Inf. Regt.	

2nd Cavalry Division (Lt.Gen. Barn Piré)

1st & 6th Chasseurs à Cheval	...	8 squadrons
5th & 6th Lancers	...	7 squadrons

Artillery

5 batteries foot artillery	
1 battery horse artillery	46 guns
Engineers	

Total infantry	...	19,750
Total cavalry	...	1,729
Total artillery	...	1,385
Total engineers	...	409

The Brunswickers formed their own brigade (commanded by the Black Duke himself) for the Waterloo campaign, and were part of Wellington's Reserve. When news of the French thrust at Quatre Bras reached Wellington, he sent part of the Reserve, including the Brunswickers, to bolster up the weak Netherlands forces there. The Brunswickers involved were:

(Left)

Senior musician, 1st Line Bn., 1815—cf. Plate H3. The Russian *kiwer* shako has a gold top band, and red cords, pompon, plume and tassels; the plate is silver, but the chin scales are gilt. Note extensive gold lacing on the black, red-faced dolman. The sabre knot is yellow and light blue, the trouser piping red. (Beyer-Pegau)

(Above and right)

Line Bn. private's shako of *kiwer* shape, 1815. The felt body, very faded now, was once black, with robust black leather top surface, top band, headband and peak, the latter edged with brass. The cockade and chin scales are black leather, the pompon light blue over yellow. (Landesmuseum Braunschweig; photos by author, and courtesy G. A. Embleton)

Avantgarde

Two companies of Gelernte Jäger	
Two companies of Light Infantry	690 men

Light Infantry Brigade

Leib-Bataillon	
1st Light Inf. Bn.	
2nd Light Inf. Bn.	2,965 men
3rd Light Inf. Bn.	

Line Infantry Brigade

1st Line Inf. Bn.	
2nd Line Inf. Bn.	2,075 men
3rd Line Inf. Bn.	

Cavalry

The Hussar Regt.	...	727 men
Uhlan Squadron	...	246 men

Artillery

One horse artillery battery, 8 guns	...	188 men
One foot artillery battery, 8 guns	...	227 men

Uhlan, 1815. The *czapka* crown; collar, cuffs, shoulder straps, plastron, and piping of the *kurtka*; the overall stripes, and the top half of the lance pennon, are all light blue. The *czapka* band and piping and bottom half of the pennon are yellow; the buttons and picker equipment, brass. Note silver death's-head badge on the lower front of the *czapka*. See text for further details, and Plate G1 for officer's uniform. (Beyer-Pegau)

Feldgendarmerie

One commando of Polizei Husaren	...	17 men

The artillery and the 1st and 3rd Light Battalions did not reach the battlefield until 6 pm that evening; but the bulk of the Brunswickers arrived on the field of Quatre Bras along the Brussels road at 2.50 pm on 16 June. By then, the Netherlands forces there had been reinforced by the following troops:

1st Brigade of the 2nd Dutch-Belgian Division of the 1st Corps (Maj.Gen. Count de Bylandt)

7th Line Regt.[1]	...	701 men
27th Jäger Bn.	...	809 men
5th Militia Bn.	...	482 men
7th Militia Bn.	...	675 men
8th Militia Bn.	...	566 men
One foot arty. bty.	...	8 guns

[1]The 7th Dutch Line Regiment, with 701 men, was part of the 1st Brigade but arrived late on the field of Quatre Bras at about 6 pm.

Fifty hussars of the 2nd Silesian Hussar Regiment (Prussian Army) had appeared on the field briefly earlier in the day, and rendered valuable service by pushing back the French outposts; but they had later returned eastwards to their parent unit, and the Prince of Orange had no cavalry under his command.

Recognising the importance of Quatre Bras, Wellington had sent the 5th Infantry Division from his reserve to bolster up the Prince of Orange's heavily pressed, but gallant force. Apart from the Brunswickers, the 5th Division, commanded by Lt.Gen. Sir Thomas Picton, included the following troops:

8th British Brigade (Maj.Gen. Sir James Kempt)

1st Bn., 28th Regt.	...	557 men
1st Bn., 32nd Regt.	...	662 men
1st Bn., 79th Regt.	...	703 men
1st Bn., 95th Regt.	...	549 men

9th British Brigade (Maj.Gen. Sir Denis Pack)

3rd Bn., 1st Regt.	...	604 men
1st Bn., 42nd Regt.	...	526 men
2nd Bn., 44th Regt.	...	455 men
1st Bn., 92nd Regt.	...	588 men

4th Hanoverian Brigade (Col. Best)

Landwehr Bn. Verden	...	621 men
Landwehr Bn. Lüneburg	...	624 men
Landwehr Bn. Osterode	...	677 men
Landwehr Bn. Münden	...	660 men

Total Infantry	7,117 men

Artillery

British Foot Battery (Maj. Rogers)
Hanoverian Foot Battery (Hauptmann von Rettberg)

At this time a violent struggle was developing around the farm of St Pierre, where the 5th Dutch Militia Bn. was holding out against heavy odds. These young militiamen finally broke under the continued assault, and the French occupied the vital farm. Now the 3rd Dutch Light Cavalry Brigade (Gen. van Merlen) arrived, and attempted to restore the situation; but the two regiments (5th Dutch Light Dragoons with 441 sabres, and the 6th Dutch Hussars with 641 sabres) were overthrown by Piré's cavalry, and pushed off the battlefield.

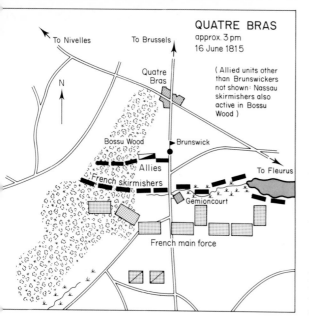

To Nivelles
To Brussels
Quatre Bras
N

(Allied units other
than Brunswickers
not shown: Nassau
skirmishers also
active in Bossu
Wood)

Bossu Wood
Brunswick
Allies
French skirmishers
To Fleurus
Germioncourt
French main force

As soon as the Brunswickers arrived they were thrown forward against the farm of St Pierre in an attempt to win back the ground lost by the Dutch. The two Gelernte Jäger companies of the Avantgarde went into Bossu Wood while the 2nd Light Battalion was sent over to the left flank of the allied position near Materne Pond. The main body of the Black Duke's force remained on the Brussels–Charleroi road.

Now the French began to push forward through Bossu Wood and the Duke of Wellington asked the Black Duke to advance towards Germioncourt and extend his right to link up with the Dutch skirmishers in Bossu Wood. The Leib-Bataillon (under Maj. Pröstler), the 1st Line Battalion (Maj. Metzner) and the two Light Infantry Companies of the Avantgarde advanced, the latter linking up in a skirmishing line with their colleagues, the Gelernte Jäger, in Bossu Wood. Directly behind the infantry were the Brunswick Hussars (Maj. Cramm) and the Uhlan Squadron (Maj. Pott). The 2nd and 3rd Line Battalions remained in front of Quatre Bras itself as a reserve.

The French were now preparing a general assault on Quatre Bras, and the 5th British Division was being subjected to a very telling cannonade. To forestall this assault Wellington decided to attack the enemy and pre-empt the French blow. Despite heavy French fire this assault by Kempt's and Pack's brigades was successful, and the French line was thrown back across the valley by Materne Pond.

Meanwhile, the French were raking the exposed Brunswickers with artillery and skirmisher fire and their losses were mounting, particularly among the Hussars. Although some veterans of the old Black Band had been taken into the newly re-formed forces of the Black Duke, they had been relatively few in number, and had been split up among all the units in order to supply cadres of experienced men around which the new recruits could be based. Thus the great majority of each battalion was made up of new, raw recruits; and this was particularly true of the Hussars and Uhlans. The Black Duke himself was very much aware of the brittle morale of his men, and he sought to maintain their spirits, despite their considerable casualties, by calmly walking up and down in front of them, smoking his pipe in the fury of the battle. He also requested some artillery from the Duke of Wellington so that he might at least reply to the enemy cannonade. Four guns were sent, and set up to the right of the Brunswickers; but two of these were quickly put out of action by well-aimed enemy fire. Now a mass of Jerome's infantry began to advance northwards along the Brussels road and extending out westwards to Bossu Wood, pushing the Dutch-Belgian and Brunswick skirmishers before them.

In an effort to impede this advance the Black Duke charged the French at the head of his Uhlan Squadron; but this faint hope was doomed by the musketry of the enemy infantry, and the Uhlans fell back with heavy losses to Quatre Bras. The advance of Jerome's troops continued, and the Brunswick infantry were also pushed back to the vital crossroads. The Leib-Bataillon was hotly pursued by the enemy, and a telling volley of artillery fire finally broke the young troops' composure: they fled back to Quatre Bras in spite of Maj. Pröstler's efforts to rally them.

It was at this point that the Black Duke, also trying to re-form his men, was struck by a musket ball which penetrated his hand, body and liver. The time was about 6 pm.

Duke Friedrich Wilhelm of Brunswick died within minutes, his only words being to his aide, Maj. von Wachholtz: 'Mein lieber Wachholtz, wo ist denn Olfermann?' ('My dear Wachholtz, where is Olfermann[1]?').

The Brunswick Hussars were now ordered forward to counter Piré's light cavalry, which was also advancing on Quatre Bras; but they, outnumbered and subjected to heavy musket fire as they advanced unsupported, were also driven back.

The Brunswickers eventually rallied at the Quatre Bras crossroads, and successfully held up further advances on this sector while on the Allied left flank the British 95th Regiment and the 2nd Brunswick Light Battalion effectively checked French outflanking attempts. The Allied cavalry being greatly inferior in numbers and quality to that of the French, the British and their allies were continuously subjected to heavy cavalry attacks. Most of these were beaten off. While Ney was still desperately trying to break the Allied line, gradual reinforcements were joining Wellington from his rear and were slowly tipping the balance in his favour, although cavalry was still scarce.

Now the Brunswick artillery and the 1st and 3rd Light Battalions arrived on the field; the guns were set up to the left of Quatre Bras, and the infantry reinforced their countrymen (the 1st and 3rd Line Battalions) in the houses of Quatre Bras. It was about 6.30 pm when the newly arrived 1st British Division was ordered into Bossu Wood which they speedily cleared of the French light troops who had threatened the British right for so long. The Brunswick Leib-Bataillon joined this advance by the British Foot Guards of Maitland's Brigade, and formed on the left of their line as they prepared to advance against the French infantry between Bossu Wood and the Charleroi road. A sudden rush of French cavalry was noticed to their flank, but both British and Brunswickers saved themselves by their cool behaviour: the British Guards simply moved into the ditch along the edge of Bossu Wood, while the Brunswickers quickly formed square and poured a deadly flanking volley into the cavalry. This was followed by more fire from the British Guards, and the shattered cavalry fled the field.

Wellington now outnumbered Ney by about 28,000 to 18,000, and he ordered a general advance which pushed the French off the field. Ney withdrew to the heights of Frasne; but Wellington did not pursue, as he had not heard of Blücher's progress at Ligny.

It had been a hard battle, and the Brunswickers had borne much of the brunt of the fighting throughout the whole long day. Siborne gives total Allied dead, wounded and missing as:

British	...	2,275
Hanoverians	...	369
Brunswickers	...	819
	Total	3,463

However, the official Brunswick despatch after the battle gives the Brunswick casualty figures for Quatre Bras as follows:

	Killed	Wounded	Total
Officers	3	23	26
Men	185	373	558
Totals	*188*	*396*	*584*

(No mention is made of missing personnel.)

Singled out for special commendation in this official report were the Leib-Bataillon, the 2nd Light Battalion and the 2nd Line Battalion.

Waterloo, 18 June 1815

Hearing finally of Blücher's defeat at Ligny, and his intended withdrawal northwards to support him in a final attempt to stop Napoleon at Waterloo, Wellington pulled his forces back from Quatre Bras during 17 June and deployed them along the ridge across the Charleroi–Brussels road at Mont St Jean—a position which he had long had in mind.

The Brunswick corps (commanded by Oberst Olfermann since the death of the Black Duke) was in the Allied Reserve, and at the start of the day they were positioned about half a mile due north of the farm of Hougoumont, in the second line of Allied troops. The left of the corps rested on the Nivelles road; the Avantgarde was detached to the right of the village of Merbe Braine. All units of the Brunswick corps were present on the field that morning. Their strength, according to Siborne, was:

Infantry	...	4,586	
Cavalry	...	866	
Artillery	...	510	with 16 guns
	Total	5,962	

[1]Olfermann was the Colonel commanding the Brunswick brigade.

The Brunswickers were split into three bodies for the duration of Waterloo. The cavalry operated with other Allied cavalry units. The Avantgarde, the Leib-Bataillon and the 1st Light Battalion were posted at the north-west corner of Hougoumont in support of the garrison there. The 2nd and 3rd Light Battalions and the three Line Battalions, together with the artillery, were initially in reserve in the second line of the Allied position.

Their immediate opponents on the western half of the battlefield were once again to be the forces under Ney whom they had fought so desperately at Quatre Bras two days before.

The battle commenced at about 11.30 am when Reille's corps began an attack on Hougoumont. It raged for about three hours before the Brunswickers were seriously involved. This was on the occasion of the first massive French cavalry attack directed against the Allied right.

The cavalry consisted of Milhaud's 24 squadrons of Cuirassiers, and Lefebvre-Desnouette's Light Cavalry Division of the Guard (seven squadrons of Red Lancers and 12 squadrons of Chasseurs à Cheval de la Garde). They ascended the slope on which the main Allied line was based, flooded over the cannon to the front of it, and pushed on to attack the Allied infantry, drawn up in squares on the reverse slope. There was general apprehension among the Allied commanders as to how these mainly raw young soldiers would conduct themselves under such a heavy attack after having suffered quite heavily at Quatre Bras only two days before. In the event, the Brunswickers behaved as well as any veteran British unit. The attack was driven off, and the Brunswick Hussars and Uhlans took part in the Allied counterattack which hastened the Frenchmen on their way out of the Allied line.

Gathering once more, the French cavalry attacked again, and a cavalry battle developed on the Allied position between part of the French assaulting force and Somerset's cavalry brigade supported by the British 23rd Light Dragoons, Trip's Dutch-Belgian Carabinier Brigade, the Brunswick Hussars and Uhlans, the 1st Light Dragoons of the King's German Legion and the British 7th Hussars. The French cavalry outnumbered the Allied units by about two to one, but this disadvantage was balanced by the fire of the

Officer of Gelernte Jägers, 1815. **Light grey uniform with dark green facings, plume and gloves; silver buttons and trim; silver and yellow sash and sabre knot; black belts and slings.** (Beyer-Pegau)

British infantry squares on the flanks and rear of the French. After a bloody fight the French fell back; and, among other regiments, the Brunswickers were commended for their bravery in this action.

The story of the repeated and augmented French cavalry charges of the afternoon is too well known to bear repeating here. The real crisis of the battle developed after these costly attacks had been abandoned. The farm of La Haye Sainte, held heroically by a garrison of Maj. Baring's King's German Legion light infantry, fell some time after 6 pm to an all-arms attack; Baring's men ran out of ammunition at a critical moment, and were overrun in fierce hand-to-hand fighting. Ney quickly exploited this success, bringing guns up to the captured buildings to fire on Wellington's front from only 200 yards' range, and sending snipers forward to harass the mauled squares in the centre of the Allied front line. A counterattack by Ompteda's KGL infantry was smashed by French heavy cavalry; and at last it seemed that

Wellington's front was about to crumble.

The Duke ordered up the Brunswickers and Chassé's Netherlands division to plug the torn centre of his front, leading the former from behind Maitland's and Adam's brigades, forward and to their left to fill the gap between Halkett's and Kruse's battered commands. They came under heavy fire, and at one point were forced back about one hundred yards. Wellington rallied them in person, whereupon they steadied. Their ammunition was soon running low, however; one battalion is reported to have run out completely. Kincaid of the 95th Rifles recalled that the Brunswickers (2nd and 3rd Light and 1st, 2nd and 3rd Line Bns.) tended to blaze away at anyone not wearing Brunswick black—an understandable reaction to the confusion and tension of close combat, bearing in mind that most were young and inexperienced. Mercer of the Royal Horse Artillery, whose battery was nearby, praised their relative steadiness under heavy fire, which impressed him more than he had been at Quatre Bras. The Brunswickers played their part in fighting off the last attack of the Imperial Guard infantry, trading fire with the 1st Bn., 3rd Foot Grenadiers. With the defeat of the Guard, and the arrival of the Prussians, the French army collapsed; and the Brunswickers took part in the general advance by the Allied army.

Siborne gives the losses of the Brunswickers at Waterloo as follows:

	Dead	Wounded	Missing
Officers	7	26	-
NCOs & men	147	430	50
Horses	77	-	-

However, according to casualty returns in the Brunswick Landesmuseum, the losses among the rank and file of the Brunswick corps engaged at Quatre Bras and Waterloo give the following totals:

	Dead	Wounded	Missing
Hussar Regt.	16	45	40
Uhlan Sqn.	4	12	15
Horse Arty. Bty.	2	4	2
Train Co.	-	1	-
Avantgarde	20	70	45
Leib-Bataillon	41	145	29
1st Light Bn.	6	31	34
2nd Light Bn.	54	110	39
3rd Light Bn.	53	160	57
1st Line Bn.	25	98	54
2nd Line Bn.	25	164	31
3rd Line Bn.	14	68	31
Foot Arty. Bty.	-	6	1
Train Co.	-	4	1
Total	*260*	*918*	*378*

Uniforms, 1809

Infantrymen (Privates)—see Plate B1:

Shako Although supplied by the Austrians, these do not seem to have been of the usual Austrian infantry pattern. According to paintings of the Brunswickers at this time, the shakos were of black felt, slightly larger at the top than at the headband and having a black leather peak, top, and top and bottom bands. A black leather chin strap was fitted, and the shako bore a white metal skull-and-crossbones badge. Above this badge was a circular black leather cockade extending to the top of the shako. The shako was surmounted by a black plume about $1\frac{1}{4}$ times higher than the body, made of horsehair on a stiff centrepiece; it was so constructed that the top of the plume was a knot of horsehair with a tuft of short hairs sticking upwards above it, long strands of horsehair drooping down from this knot and reaching the peak. (Originally there had been a black feather plume.) Some paintings show officers wearing silver chin scales, but no other special decoration on their shakos.

Coats The garment provided for the infantry of the corps was a so-called *Polrock* or *Litewka*, the national dress of Lithuania, which was to become popular among volunteer German units in 1813. It was black, single-breasted, and had skirts which reached down to just above the knee. It had a light blue standing collar, rather high (just touching the lobes of the ears) and worn open at the front in the Austrian style. The sleeves had pointed cuffs; but sources differ as to whether the infantry cuff was light blue or black.

Jurgen Olmes in Plate 76 of his series *Heere der Vergangenheit* shows an infantry private (Figure 1) and an officer (Figure 2) with light blue cuffs. A

Germany, 1809;
1: Trumpeter, Hussar Regiment
2: Officer, Hussar Regiment
3: Trooper, Uhlan Squadron

A

Germany, 1809:
1: Private, Infantry Regiment
2: Company officer, Infantry Regiment
3: Officer, Gelernte Jäger Company
4: Jäger, Gelernte Jäger Company

British service, Peninsula, 1813:
1: Trooper, Hussar Regiment
2: Officer, Hussar Regiment

C

British service, Peninsula, 1810-14:
1: Private, Brunswick-Oels Jägers
2: Company officer, Brunswick-Oels Jägers
3: Sharpshooter, detached company, Brunswick-Oels Jägers

Belgium, 1815:
1: Field officer, 1st Line Battalion, undress
2: Company officer, Leib-Bataillon, service dress
3: Drum-major, 2nd Line Battalion

Quatre Bras, 1815:
1: Jäger, Avantgarde
2: Private, Light Infantry, Avantgarde
3: Sergeant, 2nd Light Battalion
4: Private, 1st Light Battalion

F

Quatre Bras, 1815:
1: Officer, Uhlan Squadron
2: Duke of Brunswick
3: Sergeant-major, Leib-**Bataillon**

Waterloo, 1815:
1: Private, 2nd Line Battalion
2: Company officer, 1st Line Bn., with Herzogsfahne
3: Drummer, 1st Line Battalion

justification he quotes Article 5 of the Vienna Convention which laid down that the uniform of the corps was to be 'Schwarz mit lichtblauen Aufschlägen' ('black with light blue facings or cuffs'). 'Aufschlägen' is a confusing word meaning either 'cuffs' or 'facings' and, without further illustration, it is impossible to interpret.

In the 17th century the inter-regimental distinguishing colours were worn, initially, only on the cuffs of the coat, as lapels and collars often did not exist. When these latter items came into use they were often in the colour of the cuff (Aufschlag): thus 'cuff' and 'facings' are almost synonymous.

Olmes also states that other pictorial sources show these cuffs to have been black, and quotes Kortzfleisch, R. Knötel and H. Knötel. These latter sources are recognised as being extremely reliable; and to this list I would add A. Beyer-Pegau, a Saxon artist, who between 1898 and 1904 painted a series of over 100 water colours of Brunswick's troops from the 18th century up to 1870. These paintings were based on actual uniform items in the Brunswick Heimatmuseum and are approximately 12 ins. by 18 ins. in size. The detail and artistry are magnificent. Beyer-Pegau shows black cuffs, and there is no doubt that his pictures were used as source material by the Knötels. Weighing all these facts, I would think that black cuffs would be the most likely answer.

The shoulders of the *Litewka* were narrow by modern standards and the sleeves (which came up partially over the points of the shoulder) had a slightly 'puffed' appearance. No shoulder straps are shown.

The breast of the *Litewka* was covered by six rows of round black lace extending from collar to waist. Each lace was of the same length, and the outer ends terminated in black tassels. Instead of buttons, the coat was closed with six black 'toggles', as worn on modern duffle coats. There were no turnbacks on the skirts, no visible pockets and no ornamentation of any type. There was a single, central rear vent. The simplicity of the garment was probably influenced by economy and the need to produce a large quantity of uniforms in a short time.

Legwear Plain black trousers were worn with a narrow (about $\frac{1}{4}$ in. wide) light blue side stripe. Underneath these trousers were shoes and black gaiters with black buttons.

Equipment Black, Austrian-pattern cartridge pouch, without badge, on a black leather crossbelt over the left shoulder; over the right shoulder a bayonet scabbard on a similar belt. A brown calfskin pack of Austrian pattern, with three steel buckles, was carried on the back by means of two black straps over the shoulders, a connecting strap holding these together across the wearer's chest.

A grey cloth haversack was carried on a strap over the right shoulder; and the water-bottle glass, within a brown wicker-work cover on a cord over the right shoulder.

Hair and beards Hair was cut short and moustaches were worn.

Non-commissioned officers

Differences in dress between privates and NCOs were very limited and not too obvious. NCOs carried a sabre as well as a bayonet, and distinctions between junior and senior NCOs would probably have been shown by different patterns of sabre fist straps, although this is not certain. Canes as a sign of office were not carried at this date.

Officers—see Plate B2

Apart from the superior quality of their clothing and equipment officers' distinctions were limited to their silver chin scales (*if* these were generally worn); their weapons; and the fact that flanking each of the six central toggles on their chest were two other toggles situated half way towards the tassels at the outer ends of the lace.

They carried light cavalry sabres with three-bar steel hilts, black grips, black and steel sheaths and black slings; a black waist belt with silver lion's head clasps, and a silver and yellow Portepee or sabre knot. They wore white gloves.

Drummers

No explicit information concerning drummers of the Brunswick corps has been uncovered in my research, but I would assume that they wore 'swallow's nests' in light blue and black, with the senior or 'battalion' drummer having 'swallow's nests' perhaps in light blue and silver.

The Hussar Regiment: Troopers—cf. Plate A1

Shako As for the infantry but with brass chin scales.

Dolman This was black, with a light blue collar of infantry dimensions, and pointed, light blue cuffs which were sewn only on to the outside of the

Gelernte Jäger of the Avantgarde, 1815—see details in text, and Plate F1. (Beyer-Pegau)

sleeves, the inner side of the sleeve being black; above the cuffs were black Hungarian knots. The dolman extended only to the waist, and the chest bore 14 rows of round black lace and five rows of spherical, black glass buttons. There were no tassels at the ends of the rows of lace. The seams on the back of the dolman and sleeves were decorated with round black lace. There were no shoulder straps.

Legwear Most pictures of hussars show black overalls with leather inserts, brass buttons and a narrow, light blue side piping. Screw-in, straight-necked steel spurs were worn. The hussar boots were worn under the overalls.

Sash A yellow cord waist sash with light blue barrels was worn; it had a yellow whip and tassel fringes, with light blue runners and tassel body.

Equipment The pouch belt was black leather with brass rosette, chains and oval picker plate; the pouch was of black leather bearing a white metal skull-and-crossbones. The sabre was of Austrian light cavalry pattern with a steel hilt, black grip, black leather fist strap, steel sheath, and black sling and waist belt with a simple steel snake clasp. Sabretasches were of plain black leather and hung on three straps.

Greatcoats When made up these were of light drab 'pepper and salt' cloth, mid-calf length, with a high collar and a cape extending to just above the wrist.

NCOs

As with the infantry battalions, NCOs' distinction are unclear but were probably displayed on the sabre strap.

Trumpeters—see Plate A1

Beyer-Pegau shows a trumpeter of hussars in 1809 and the deviations in dress from that of a trooper are as follows: 'swallow's nests' in gold and black with a gold fringe along the bottom (perhaps Beyer-Pegau painted the regimental trumpeter); white gloves and a brass trumpet with light blue and yellow cords and tassels.

Officers—see Plate A2

Shako as for officers of infantry. Instead of a dolman, hussar officers wore the same pattern of black *Polrock* or *Litewka* as infantry officers, but on the chest were six rows of round black lace ending in black tassels. The *Polrock* was closed by six black toggles; the collar was light blue, the cuffs black.

Around their waists officers wore yellow silk hussar-pattern sashes with silver barrels, runners and tassel. Pouch belt and pouch were as for the troopers but of better quality, and the officer's black sabretasche was decorated with a silver skull-and-crossbones badge. Their black waist belt had lion's heads flanking the 'snake' and the sabre was carried in a black and steel sheath on black slings. The sabre knot was as for infantry officers. White gloves.

Legwear was black overalls, having a narrow light blue side piping, buttons on the sides, and black leather reinforcement. These were worn over hussar boots with short, straight-necked, screw-in spurs.

Horse furniture Harness was of black leather, Hungarian pattern, with white metal fittings. Other ranks had black sheepskin saddle covers with light blue wolf's-tooth edging; and officers had black cloth shabraques, with pointed rear corners, having a wide edging of light blue. Saddles were of the old Turkish or 'Bock' type, being made of birch wood and leather.

The Horse Artillery Battery: Gunners

Hats Infantry-pattern shakos

Coats Short *Kollets* in black with six rows of round black lace on the chest and three rows of black glass buttons. The standing collar, Polish cuffs, shoulder straps and skirt turnbacks were light blue.

Trousers As for Hussars

Equipment As for Hussars

Officers

Infantry officer's shako, Hussar officer's coat (*Polrock*), black pouch belt bearing a gold, heart-shaped cartouche charged with the ducal cypher ('FW'). Sash as for Hussar officers; legwear and equipment as for Hussar officers. White gloves.

Horse furniture Harness and saddles as for the Hussars; black cloth shabraques with pointed rear corners and light blue edging.

Guns and limbers were painted grey.

Troops raised during the 1809 campaign:

During the Brunswickers' occupation of Leipzig, a 'Gelernte Jäger -oder Scharfschützen- Kompanie' ('Experienced Rifle or Sharpshooter Company') was raised. On 23 June 1809 it had a strength of four officers and 180 Jägers.

The uniform was a curious mixture of Prussian and Austrian items, the coat being very similar to that worn by the Prussian Füsiliers of this period while their hats were Austrian Jäger pattern.

Jägers—see Plate B4

Hat Black Corsican hat with wide green headband and green edge trim, with the left hand brim extended and turned up so that it was higher than the crown of the hat. Apparently no badge, cockade or other decoration.

Coat Dark green, double-breasted, closed with two parallel rows each of nine yellow buttons. Collar, cuffs, shoulder straps and skirt turnbacks were red. The collar was standing and open at the front, and the cuffs were straight (Swedish) pattern having two buttons in the rear top corner.

Trousers Long grey or white trousers worn over shoes and black gaiters.

Equipment White-handled sword-bayonet (Hirsch-fänger) in a black leather sheath carried on the left hip on a black cross belt over the right shoulder. Personal effects were carried in a black leather satchel (Ranzentasche) in the same position. Over

Hornist of the Gelernte Jäger companies, 1815. Uniform as for riflemen, with added dark green and silver 'swallow's nests'; brass horn with yellow and dark green cords; grey greatcoat; brass-hilted sword bayonet. (Beyer-Pegau)

the right shoulder was a green cord which carried the brown, brass-fitted powder horn. The short rifle had a light brown sling.

Officers of Jägers—see Plate B3

Hat Infantry officer's shako with skull-and-crossbones badge, but instead of the black horsehair plume, they had a drooping plume made of black cock's feathers. White gloves.

Coat Long-skirted green frock coat with a woven gold aiguillette on the right shoulder; buttons and facings as for the Jägers.

Trousers Long grey trousers with red side stripes worn over shoes.

Equipment Waist belt and sabre as for infantry officers.

From 16–21 July 1809, in Schleiz, the formation of a third battalion of infantry, called the '**3rd or Freien Jäger-Bataillon**', was begun. The process of formation was continued in Zwickau on 22–23 July 1809. This unit had two companies. The uniform of this 3rd Battalion was as for the 1st and

2nd Battalions except that the facings were yellow, and the officers wore a golden aiguillette on the right shoulder. To this battalion 300 'turned' prisoners of the 5th Westfalian Infantry Regiment were later added.

Uhlan Squadron: Troopers—see Plate A3

The formation of this unit was begun in Dresden, and the squadron joined the Duke's forces at Zwickau on 23 July 1809. Their uniform was almost an exact copy of that worn by the Austrian 'Graf von Meerveldt' Uhlanen-Regiment, about the only difference being the small white metal skull-and-crossbones badge worn on the lower part of the front of the *Czapka*.

Hat Square-topped *Czapka* having a yellow upper part and a black leather lower part and peak. No cockade or plume, but a white metal skull-and-crossbones badge on the lower front of the black headband, and yellow cords and 'flounders'.

Coat Typical lancer *Kurtka* of traditional Polish pattern, in dark green with ponceau red facings (collar, pointed cuffs, lapels, shoulder straps, turnbacks and piping to rear of sleeves and back of jacket), and yellow buttons.

Trousers Dark green overalls with narrow red piping, yellow buttons and black leather reinforcements. Under these were worn black boots with short, straight-necked, screw-in spurs.

Equipment Around the waist was worn a wide dark green and red girdle (*Passgürtel*), and under the jacket was a black leather waist belt supporting a sabre of the pattern carried by the Hussars. The pouch belt and pouch were also of Hussar pattern, and armament was augmented by a long, brown wooden lance with steel head and shoe and a red and yellow pennant. Apparently the Uhlans did not carry carbines.

Officers

Generally as for the men, but of better quality; the major differences were that instead of the red shoulder straps of the men the officers had gold epaulettes, and at the rear of the waist was the so-called 'waterfall' made up of gold tassels. White gloves.

Horse furniture Black harness with white metal fittings as for the Hussars; 'Bock' saddles; green shabraques edged in red and having long, pointed rear corners.

General Notes

Fatigue caps were worn by all ranks, and took the form of a beret-like cap with light blue headband about two inches wide and a floppy black crown. Apparently the officers distinguished themselves from the men by having silver decoration around the light blue headband and the Black Duke himself had a band of silver laurel leaves above the blue headband, though sources vary as to the exact design—see Plate G2. One source at least shows a Hussar officer wearing this cap with a silver skull-and-crossbones badge on the band, and a silver tassel from the centre of the very baggy crown: see Suhr painting accompanying the text.

The 1st Battalion of the infantry regiment had a band, and in 1809 Queen Sophie Charlotte of England presented Duke Friedrich Wilhelm with a 'Schellenbaum' or 'Jingling Johnny' for this band. This instrument was later carried by the Brunswick Infantry Regiment No. 92 until 1918, and has been in the Brunswick Landesmuseum since it was presented by the officers of the regiment after the Second World War. This Schellenbaum is unusual in that the horns of the crescent turn downwards instead of up, as is the case with all other Schellenbäume of the German Army. Originally the tips of the crescent carried red horse tails but these were later replaced by the black ones which can still be seen today. Until 1815 the Black Band carried no flags or standards.

Uniforms in English Service, 1810-15

Although certain minor items of equipment and uniform changed from being of Austrian to English style, the main colour scheme of the Black Band's uniforms was retained. They received the English system of rank badges for other ranks, consisting of white or silver stripes on the upper right arm; English canvas packs, water-bottles, pouches, muskets and bayonets. Officers adopted the British crimson silk net waist sash and the gold and crimson sword knot, and their appointments bore the cypher 'GR'.

Infantry: Privates—see Plate D1

Shako As for privates in 1809.

Coat The *Polrock* now gave way to a short, dolman-like tunic in black, with black cuffs, light blue collar, and black lace and toggles on the chest.

Trousers Black with narrow light blue side piping, worn over short black gaiters.

Equipment Brown-painted canvas pack decorated with a white springing horse below a motto in black NUNQUAM RETRORSUM. Grey greatcoat rolled on top of the pack; black cross belts carrying a plain black pouch and a black bayonet scabbard. Round wooden British-style water-bottle painted light blue and bearing the white initials 'B.L.J.' ('Braunschweig Lauenburg'sche Jäger'). White canvas haversack; British musket with brown sling.

NCOs

Rank badges in English style, i.e. white or silver chevrons on the upper right sleeve; waist sashes in crimson with a light blue central stripe; sabres as well as bayonets, otherwise as for privates.

Drummers

As for privates but with 'swallow's nests' in light blue and black; no pouch or musket, and a sabre instead of a bayonet. Drum bandolier and apron black, drumsticks black held in a square brass plate

Surviving 'Corsican' hat, as worn by the Jäger and Light Infantry companies of the Avantgarde, 1815. Trim, band and plume are dark green, while the faded felt body was once black. The horse badge is silver. Note that Knötel's plate in *Uniformenkunde Vol. IV* shows the wrong side of the brim turned up. (Landesmuseum Braunschweig; photos by author, and courtesy G. A. Embleton)

on the bandolier; brass drum with light blue and yellow hoops.

Officers—see Plate D2

Shako As for infantry officers of 1809.

Coat This was a Hussar-style dolman with no skirts; five rows of black buttons and 14 rows of black lace on the chest; black cuffs; light blue collar with black embroidery. Their badges of office consisted of a crimson silk waist sash in the light infantry style, and a gold and crimson sabre knot.

Trousers Black overalls with a narrow light blue side seam worn over short boots.

Equipment Hussar sabre in steel sheath on black slings as in 1809. White gloves were worn.

Sharpshooters: Privates—see Plate D3

Shako As for privates of infantry.

Coat Dark green single-breasted tunic with light blue collar and light blue Polish cuffs; very short light blue turnbacks; a single row of yellow buttons.

Trousers Light grey with narrow light blue piping, worn over short black gaiters.

Equipment Pack, pouch, haversack and belts as for privates of infantry; British Baker rifle with brown sling and sword bayonet.

Officers

All items as for officers of infantry, but dolmans in the dark green cloth of the Sharpshooters instead of black, and grey overalls instead of black.

The Hussars: Troopers—see Plate C1

Apart from the differences noted here, the uniform in British service was almost identical to that worn in 1809. The waist sash was now light blue and crimson; the black pouch belt had no picker equipment; instead of overalls the men wore black hussar breeches inside hussar boots decorated with

Officer, Light Infantry of the Avantgarde, 1815. Black uniform with dark green facings, plume and gloves; silver hat trim; silver and yellow sash and sabre knot. See text for further details, and cf. Plate F2. (Beyer-Pegau)

a black tassel and having steel screw-in spurs. A black pelisse was worn; it had black fur edging, three rows of black buttons, and 14 rows of black lace.

NCOs

As for troopers, but with silver chevrons on the upper right arm.

Trumpeters

As for troopers but with silver and light blue 'swallow's nests'.

Officers—see Plate C2

Shako As in 1809, but with a wide gold lace band around the top.

Dolman Black, with light blue cuffs and collar decorated with black lace; five rows of black buttons and 14 rows of black lace on the chest; black Hungarian knots above the cuffs; black lace embroidery to the rear seams.

Pelisse As for the dolman but with a black fur edging.

Breeches Black, with black Hungarian knots on the thighs, worn inside hussar boots having a gold top trim and tassels, and short, screw-in steel spurs.

Equipment Black pouch belt with gold picker equipment bearing the cypher 'GR'; gold and crimson waist sash, gold and crimson sabre knot; sabre, sabretasche and slings as for 1809; white gloves.

Horse furniture Black hussar harness with white metal fittings; black sheepskin saddle cover with light blue wolf's-tooth edging; Beyer-Pegau shows a black saddle cloth edged light blue with a white or silver skull-and-crossbones in the rear corner.

No mention is made of any artillery attached to the Brunswickers in Spain and it can be assumed that from 1809 until 1814 no artillery existed within the corps.

Uniforms at Waterloo, 1815

The Gelernte Jäger: Privates—see Plate F1

Hat Austrian-pattern black felt Corsican hat with green hat band and edging to brim, the left hand brim turned up. This bore a green feather tuft over a green loop, white button and, above the button and within the loop, a white metal badge in the form of a Saxon running horse. Black chinstrap[1].

Coat Short skirted, single-breasted light grey coat with green standing collar, shoulder straps, Swedish cuffs and turnbacks; white metal buttons.

Trousers Light grey, with twin green stripes down the sides; worn over shoes and black gaiters.

Equipment Black leather cross belt with a white metal frame buckle on the chest, supporting a black pouch. Hirschfänger as in 1809. Powder horn on thick green cord over the left shoulder. Brown calfskin pack with black leather straps; round tin water-bottle. Rifle with black sling.

NCOs

As for privates, but with silver rank chevrons on the upper right arm as in British service in the Peninsula: corporal, two; sergeant, three; colour sergeant, three chevrons below a crown; sergeant major, four chevrons below a crown.

Hornists

As for privates but with green 'swallow's nests' with silver edging (senior hornist with silver fringes); no pouch or rifle.

Officers

Hat Same style as for privates but with silver hat band and edging, and a drooping dark green cock's-feather plume.

Coat Cut as for privates; no shoulder straps; silver lace edging to green collar and cuffs.

Trousers Grey with double green side stripes.

Equipment Black leather pouch belt with silver picker equipment; black pouch with silver 'FW' on the lid. Silver and yellow waist sash; steel hilted hussar-pattern sabre in steel sheath on black slings; silver and yellow Portepee. Green gloves.

Light Infantry Companies of the Avantgarde —see Plate F2

These two companies, which were musket-armed rather than riflemen, are shown by Beyer-Pegau as wearing the same black infantry uniform as the Leib-Bataillon (see below) but with green collars, shoulder straps and pointed cuffs. They also wore the Corsican hat like the Gelernte Jägers, but with a

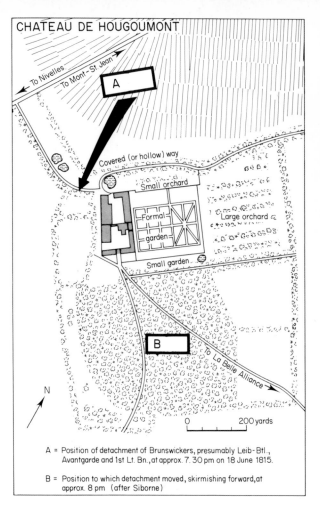

CHATEAU DE HOUGOUMONT

A = Position of detachment of Brunswickers, presumably Leib-Btl., Avantgarde and 1st Lt. Bn., at approx. 7.30 pm on 18 June 1815.

B = Position to which detachment moved, skirmishing forward, at approx. 8 pm (after Siborne)

silver bugle horn badge replacing the running horse. NCOs' and officers' distinctions seem to have been identical to those of the Jäger companies. The privates wore the same cross belts, packs and bayonets as the infantry battalions. In these, as in all other units, the sources suggest a mixed issue of muskets: both British, and either Prussian or French, can be made out.

The Leib-Bataillon: Privates

Hat Shako of the 1809 infantry style with drooping horsehair plume, black cockade, white loop and button, silver skull-and-crossbones badge, brass bosses and chinscales. The top of the shako and the bottom rim were of black leather, the rest of black felt.

Coat Black with light blue facings shown on collar and shoulder straps. This coat was of the same dolman style as worn in Spain.

Trousers Black with light blue side piping, and worn

---

[1]Knötel in his Plate 52, Volume IV of the *Uniformkunde* shows the Gelernte Jäger in 1815 as having the right hand brim of their hats turned up, and not the left. Close inspection of an actual example of the hat in the Brunswick Landesmuseum shows that the running horse badge and the bow of the green hat band are so placed that if the hat were worn the correct way round, the upturned brim would be on the left. Many subsequent artists have used Knötel as a source, thus this apparent mistake has been broadcast.

over black shoes and gaiters.

Equipment Black leather cross belts, plain black pouch, bayonet in black sheath, musket with black sling.

NCOs—see Plate G3, and cf. Plate F3

Rank badges in silver on the upper right arm as for the Gelernte Jäger; sabres in black sheaths; yellow waist sash with light blue edges and central stripe, blue runners and tassels to yellow 'whip'. The brass hilt of the sabre carried a blue and yellow sabre knot. Instead of a large cartridge pouch on a cross belt, the NCOs had a smaller pouch in plain black leather worn on a narrow black waist belt at the front centre of the body, hanging over the waist sash. Corporals did not wear the waist sash. Sergeants and above wore white gloves. For further comments, see commentary on Plate G3, and photograph on p. 9.

Drummers

As for privates except that they had 'swallow's nests' at each shoulder in light blue and black; wore no pouch or pouch belt; had sabres in black sheaths with yellow and blue sabre knots; and carried their drums on black bandoliers having an oval brass plate to hold the brass-fitted black drum sticks. The drums were brass-bodied, the hoops striped light blue and yellow, the tensioning cords white, the carrying strap and drum apron black.

Officers—see Plate E2

As for privates except no equipment; silver and yellow waist sash; instead of the short tunic they wore true black dolmans with five rows of buttons, and fine black embroidery to collar, cuffs and rear seams. They carried cavalry-pattern sabres in steel sheaths on black slings with silver and yellow sabre knots, and wore white gloves.

Majors and above had silver knots embroidered above their cuffs in place of the black knots of company officers; and they also wore black pouch belts with silver pickers and a black pouch with the silver cypher 'FW'.

The Light and Line Battalions

Apart from the differences listed here, these six units wore identical uniforms.

The three Light Battalions had a shako plate in the shape of a silver bugle horn depending from an oval cartouche bearing the number of the battalion. The three Line Battalions' shako plates took the form of an almost semi-circular 'Amazon shield' under a cartouche bearing the battalion number; on the plate was the running horse of Lower Saxony below the motto 'NUNQUAM RETRORSUM'. The facings of these units were as follows:

> 1st Light Battalion—Buff (until 1 July 1815, then rose red)
> 2nd Light Battalion—Yellow
> 3rd Light Battalion—Orange
> 1st Line Battalion—Red
> 2nd Line Battalion—Green
> 3rd Line Battalion—White

Privates—see Plates F4 and H1

Shako As for the Leib-Bataillon but with the plate as described above; instead of the horsehair plume there was a small, carrot-shaped pompon about 4 ins. high, equally divided light blue over yellow for the Line Battalions, and yellow over light blue for the Light Battalions. Partially concealed behind the white metal oval showing the battalion number was a circular black leather cockade. Black leather chin strap. From examples of actual shakos in the Brunswick Landesmuseum, it is clear that various types were in simultaneous use in the period 1813–1816; and Beyer-Pegau reflects this. Some were of the 1812 Russian *kiwer* type with the concave top, and others were flat-topped, more the Prussian model.

Tunic Short, black, reaching to waist level and having no skirts; facings shown on the standing collar and the shoulder straps only. The tunic closed by a single row of ten black glass buttons, and across the chest ten rows of doubled-round black lace ended in small tassels. False pockets were outlined in lace under each arm, and the back of the tunic was decorated with black lace. Pointed black cuffs were outlined in black lace.

Trousers, and Equipment As for the Leib-Bataillon, that is with a piping in the facing colour down the trousers.

NCOs

Badges, weapons, gloves and equipment as for NCOs of the Leib-Bataillon; shako decorations as for privates of their battalions.

Officers—see Plate H2, and see Plate E1 for undress uniform

Badges, weapons and equipment as for officers of the Leib-Bataillon. Shako: plate as for privates of their battalions, with 4 in. cut feather plume halved light blue and yellow, as privates' pompons. Gloves were green in the Light Battalions, white in the Line.

Drummers—see Plate H3, and see Plate E3 for Drum Major

Shakos as for privates; 'swallow's nests' in black and the facing colour (the 'battalion drummer' had them in the facing colour and gold); drum, bandolier and apron as described for the Leib-Bataillon. All other details as for privates of their battalions.

The Hussars

The uniforms of 1809 were retained completely except that the cuffs of the dolman were now also black. Badges of rank were silver chevrons on the upper right arm.

The Uhlan Squadron—see Plate G1 for officer's uniform

The cut and style of the uniform were exactly as for the Uhlans of 1809, but the colours had changed as follows:

Czapka Black lower half and black, brass-edged peak; light blue top half, divided from the lower half by a yellow band. The light blue top was edged in yellow piping up the corners and across the top.

Kurtka Black, with light blue collar, shoulder straps, lapels, cuffs, turnbacks and piping to rear of sleeves and body. Yellow buttons; black *Passgürtel* edged light blue.

Breeches Black, with a single wide light blue stripe for troopers, twin light blue stripes for officers.

Lance Black, with light-blue-over-yellow pennant.

Horse furniture Black shabraque and round portmanteau, both edged in light blue. Black harness, steel fittings.

Officers' *czapkas* had gold lace dividing bands between top and bottom halves, and silver cords and 'flounders'. For parades officers wore tall drooping feather plumes, light blue over yellow. A contemporary portrait exists showing an officer of Uhlans in 1815 *kurtka* and breeches but with an 1809 *czapka* (i.e. with a yellow top). In 1815 officers wore fringeless epaulettes on both shoulders, the epaulettes having light blue straps and gilt crescents and being held by silver straps and gold buttons. Their pouch belts were now gold with silver picker equipment and buckles; the pouches black with gilt

Painting by Lebrecht purporting to show the Leib-Bataillon, 1st Light Bn. and Avantgarde in action in the environs of Hougoumont on the Allied right flank at Waterloo. The colour of the Leib-Btl. is illustrated. Details of this action are not clear. Siborne states that at some point during the afternoon or early evening, when the 2nd Bn., 2nd Foot Guards moved from their reserve position just north-west of Hougoumont into the chateau itself, some Brunswick units took their place. At about 8 pm some Brunswickers were apparently skirmishing forward through Hougoumont woods; but this scenario of men lining a wall with timber firing steps and loopholes seems to be inconsistent with the known facts. An interesting anecdote from Siborne quotes Capt. Ross of the British 51st Foot to the effect that some Brunswick stragglers attached themselves to his company, fighting with them for much of the 18th, and that these included 'old sweats' who remembered Ross from the Peninsula—and so, presumably, were from the Leichte-Brigade.

edging and cypher 'FW'. Sashes were silver and yellow, as were the sabre knots; all other items as for 1809.

NCOs' rank badges consisted of one or two silver reversed chevrons following the top of the cuffs.

The Artillery: Privates

Shako This was of Hussar pattern. The foot artillery wore a brass grenade on the front under a round black cockade surmounted by a yellow, pear-shaped woollen pompon about 4 ins. high; and a black leather peak and chin strap. The horse artillery had a white skull-and-crossbones badge, and instead of a pompon they had a drooping black horsehair plume.

Tunic This was of infantry cut for the foot artillery and dolman-style for the horse artillery. Both were black, with black collar and cuffs outlined in yellow, and black buttons, lace and tassels. Rank badges were as for the infantry but in yellow or gold.

Trousers Black with a yellow piping. Foot artillery wore black gaiters and shoes, horse artillery wore hussar-style overalls.

Equipment Foot artillery had a brass-hilted sabre in a black sheath on a black cross belt; horse artillery had hussar-pattern sabres on black slings.

Officers

Horse artillery officers dressed exactly as for officers of Hussars with the following exceptions: black collar and Polish cuffs edged in gold lace and embroidery; yellow trouser stripe. Foot artillery officers dressed as for horse artillery officers with the following exceptions: the shako badge was a gilt grenade, and a short yellow cut-feather plume was worn. No pouch belt or pouch was worn by officers below the rank of major; and no spurs.

The Train

Drivers of the Foot Artillery Train wore foot artillery shakos, and tunics of infantry cut in a drab dark brown/grey cloth with black collars and cuffs edged in yellow. Dark brown/grey overalls had black leather reinforcements and yellow side piping. They carried hussar sabres on black slings, and wore hussar-style spurs.

Drivers of the Horse Artillery Train wore hussar shakos of the Russian *Kiwer* model, but with a yellow grenade on the front instead of the white skull-and-crossbones. The black tunic had black collar, cuffs and turnbacks all edged in yellow; yellow grenades in the four turnback corners; black braid decoration to the rear seams of the jacket, and black braid shoulder straps. A black pouch belt had yellow fittings, and supported a black pouch with a yellow grenade badge. Black overalls bore narrow yellow pipings and black leather reinforcement, and were worn over short boots with steel, screw-in spurs. The brass-hilted sabre had a steel sheath with black leather slings and fist strap.

The Reserve Battalions

Black Corsican hats, as for the Gelernte Jäger but with black edging, no plume, and with the silver horse of lower Saxony on the upturned flap. Short black tunics had black collars and cuffs edged in white; the black trousers had a narrow white piping; and black equipment and bayonet sheath were worn. NCOs and officers wore rank distinctions as for the infantry battalions of the Line.

The Flags of the Brunswickers at Waterloo

On 18 March 1814 the ladies of Brunswick presented the Black Duke with six embroidered flags, which were presented on 12 April 1814 to the three Line Battalions. No other Brunswick units received flags. These six flags were entirely different from one another:

1. Linien-Bataillon: *(later 1st Bn. 92nd Infantry Regiment)*

Herzogsfahne Obverse, yellow bearing a wide upright light blue cross, in the centre the springing silver horse, above the horse the inscription *Sieg oder Tod* ('Victory or Death'), below the horse two crossed swords between palm leaves, in the four corners the silver cypher 'FW' and above it an oak wreath both enclosed in the eternal silver snake biting its own tail.

Reverse, divided into three equal horizontal stripes yellow, light blue, yellow; in the blue stripe the ducal arms, in the four corners the crowned silver cypher 'FW' within silver laurels.

Bataillonsfahne (later carried by the 2nd Bn., 92nd Infantry Regiment)

Obverse, yellow containing a light blue lozenge (the peaks touching the edges) bearing the ducal arms; in the four corners the crowned silver cypher 'FW'.

Reverse, yellow with a light blue lozenge (as obverse) bearing the springing horse in silver in its centre, with the silver inscription *Mit Gott für Fürst und Vaterland*, in the four corners silver horns.

2. Linien-Bataillon:

Herzogsfahne Obverse divided into three equal horizontal stripes light blue, yellow, light blue; in the yellow part a central black diamond flanked by cyphers and ducal crowns and containing the inscription *Mit Gott für Fürst und Vaterland 1813.*

Reverse, divided into three equal horizontal stripes as for the obverse but with a black field in the centre, edged in silver and bearing the springing white horse on a red ground surrounded by palm and laurel leaves. No corner emblems.

Bataillonsfahne Obverse in three equal horizontal stripes light blue, black, light blue; in the black stripe the ducal crest surrounded on the lower half by a silver laurel wreath and on the top half by the

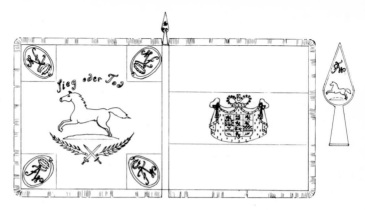

Herzogsfahne of the 1st Line Bn., 1815, with final—see text description, and Plate H2.

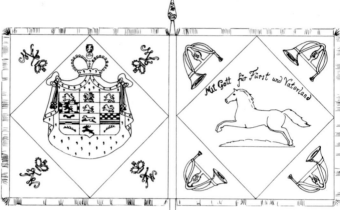

Bataillonsfahne of the 1st Line Bn., 1815—see text description.

Herzogsfahne and finial, 3rd Line Bn., 1815—see text description.

silver inscription *Ist Gott für uns, wer mag wider uns seyn.* No corner badges.

Reverse, same basic pattern and colours as obverse with golden crowned cypher 'FW' within silver laurels as the centre piece; no corner badges.

3. Linien-Bataillon:

Herzogsfahne (later carried by the 3rd Bn., 92nd Infantry Regiment) This flag was the same on both sides: light blue with the white springing horse as centre piece under a ducal crown; above the crown and horse the inscription NUNQVAM RETRORSVM. Beneath the horse an oak and a laurel twig. In the corners the silver, crowned cypher 'FW'.

Bataillonsfahne Obverse, black with a square yellow centre containing the silver inscription *Mit Gott für Fürst und Vaterland 1814* within silver oak leaves and

Fur-trimmed *Polrock* attributed to the 'Black Duke'. (Landes-museum Braunschweig, photo courtesy G. A. Embleton)

under a ducal crown. At the bottom of the wreath a silver skull-and-crossbones. No corner emblems.

Reverse, black with a light blue central square bearing the springing horse in silver with the golden inscription across the top NUNQUAM RETRORSUM. No corner emblems.

The staff tips and bandoliers of the flags were also different from one another. Both flags of the 1st Line Bn. had gilt tips bearing the springing horse of Lower Saxony and the ducal cypher, and a 'Banderole' or cravat in silver worked with round yellow cords. These two flags also had an edging of silver fringes. The flags of the 2nd and 3rd Line Bns. had staff tips of a gold crown above the pierced cypher 'FW' and the date *1814*. (Later, when the Bataillonsfahne of the 2nd Battalion was renewed, this date became *1818*, and the Herzogsfahne of the 2nd Battalion bore *1824*.) The cravats of these flags were golden with light blue round silk cord decoration; and the four flags themselves were edged with a narrow silver lace. All flag staffs were brown.

Sources used in the preparation of this book:

Bain, N.	*A Detailed Account of the Battles of Quatre Bras, Ligny and Waterloo* (Edinburgh, 1819)
Beyer-Pegau, A.	*Collection of watercolours in the Brunswick Landesmuseum*
Boulger, D. C.	*The Belgians at Waterloo* (London 1901)
Fiebig, E.	*Unsterbliche Treue* (Berlin, 1936)
Herold, J. C.	*The Battle of Waterloo* (London, 1967)
Knötel, R.	Uniform Plates 32 and 33, Vol I; 52 and 53, Vol IV; 28, Vol V; 18, Vol XVII
Knötel-Sieg	*Handbuch der Uniformkunde* (Hamburg, 1966)
Olmes, J.	*Armies of the Past*, Plate 76
Pflugk-Harttung	*Belle-Alliance (Verbundetes Heer)* (Berlin, 1915)
Schirmer, F.	*Die Zinnfigur* Neue folge, 8. Jahrgang. Heft 8/15 (August 1959)
Siborne	*The Waterloo Campaign 1815* (Birmingham, 1894)

Zeitschrift fur Heereskunde

Exhibits and documents in the Brunswick Landes-museum, the Elberfeld Collection and the Lipper-heide Collection.

The Plates

In most cases the usual full descriptive notes to the Plates are not felt necessary in this book, since individual Plate subjects are cross-referenced to detailed descriptions of uniform practice in the previous chapter. These notes are, in consequence, limited to simple identification except in those few cases where the uniform is not covered in the body text.

Germany, 1809:

A1: Trumpeter, Hussar Regiment (see pp. 33–34)
A2: Officer, Hussar Regiment (see p. 34)
A3: Trooper, Uhlan Squadron (see p. 36)

B1: *Private, Infantry Regiment* (see pp. 24, 33)
B2: *Company officer, Infantry Regiment* (see p. 33)
B3: *Officer, Gelernte Jäger Company* (see p. 35)
B4: *Jäger, Gelernte Jäger Company* (see p. 35)

British service, Peninsula, 1813:
C1: *Trooper, Hussar Regiment* (see p. 38)
C2: *Officer, Hussar Regiment* (see p. 38)

British Service, Peninsula, 1810–14:
D1: *Private, Brunswick-Oels Jägers* (see p. 37)
D2: *Company officer, Brunswick-Oels Jägers* (see p. 37)
D3: *Sharpshooter, Brunswick-Oels Jägers* (see p. 37)

It is presumed that the Sharpshooters were those three detached companies which served away from the main body of the regiment, in the brigades of the British 4th and 5th Divisions: there is no other logical explanation for their dispersal in this way, which follows the pattern seen with other skirmishing units in Wellington's army.

During the Peninsular campaign the regiment had some difficulty in recruiting up to strength. Inevitably, the purely national character of the

Two 'portraits' of the Duke of Brunswick, the full figure from Ackermann's *Repository of Arts*, Issue 16. The difficulties of accurate reconstruction of his costume at Quatre Bras are discussed under Plate G2. (Courtesy Philip Haythornthwaite)

Brunswick corps became somewhat diluted. The only regular source of new German-speaking recruits was by enlistment of prisoners of war from the many German and other eastern European units serving with the French armies in Spain. Before long a fairly motley crowd of Germans, Poles, Swiss, Scandinavians and even Croats was to be found in the ranks of the regiment, which enjoyed a rather hard-bitten reputation among the British troops. Doubtless the cadres of veteran Brunswick NCOs kept these uncertain volunteers to their duty. The regiment were known to the redcoats as the 'Brunswick Owls', in simple mispronunciation of their title; and Private James Gunn of the 42nd Highlanders rather pleasantly referred to their shako badge as 'a scalped face and shin-bone'! The Brunswickers came under strong suspicion at one stage of having eaten the 95th Rifles' dog mascot. (But it is only fair to add that other units were also accused of this crime. Of course, there may have been a *series* of dogs, consumed at intervals . . .)

Although the uniform illustrated is the regulation pattern, it may be assumed that under campaign conditions a good deal of standard British issue would have replaced worn-out items, e.g. grey or brown campaign trousers, etc.

Belgium, 1815:

E1: Field officer, 1st Line Battalion, undress uniform
Beyer-Pegau illustrates this peaked *mütze* as officer's undress headgear, without visible variation between company and field ranks. The regulation dolman is worn open over a waistcoat in unit facing

Gunner of Horse Artillery, 1815, by Beyer-Pegau. The black uniform is faced black, with yellow piping and grenade badges, a brass shako grenade, buff pouch belt and sabre knot, and yellow cord decoration on shoulder and collar. This rendering seems highly suspect; the odd collar and shoulder detail recalls that worn by Brunswick artillery in the mid-19th century, and does not figure in the written description—see relevant paragraph in body of text.

colour, lavishly laced in silver: an example of a surviving uniform will be found among the photographs. Field rank is indicated by the silver— rather than black—knots embroidered above the cuffs. The field officer's pouch belt does not seem to have been worn with undress, according to Beyer-Pegau. Green gloves were fashionable, and in undress were probably not rigidly limited to Light Bn. officers.

E2: Company officer, Leib-Bataillon, service dress (see p. 40)
E3: Drum major, 2nd Line Battalion

F1: Jäger of the Avantgarde (see pp. 38–39)
F2: Private, Light Infantry Companies of the Avantgarde (see p. 39)
F3: Sergeant, 2nd Light Battalion (see p. 40)
F4: Private, 1st Light Battalion (see p. 40)

G1: Officer, Uhlan Squadron (see p. 41)
G2: Friedrich-Wilhelm, Duke of Brunswick-Lüneburg and Oels
This attempt to reconstruct the duke's appearance at Quatre Bras is frankly speculative—many contradictory versions of his costume have been published, all of them based on posthumous material of dubious value. We base this largely on a posthumous portrait print by Carl Schröder the Elder, which does seem to be supported to some extent by other contemporary material and by surviving items in the Brunswick Landesmuseum; but we make no exaggerated claims for its accuracy.

The duke is shown at various stages in his career wearing large moustaches and sidewhiskers; here we follow a Hourtelle plate in suggesting that on the day of his death, at least, his lip was shaven. The famous but problematic cap is clearly based on a Hussar Regiment officer's undress cap, with a band of some kind of silver-on-black laurel leaf decoration above the pale blue band. We follow Schröder, who is to some extent supported by an earlier naif print, in showing this band of decoration as being *overlaid* on the blue, leaving only a narrow strip of it showing below. The Schröder print strongly hints at the rondel of silver lace on the top centre of the cap crown, but the silver tassel which might be expected to hang from it is not visible in the print, though it may well be present.

The *Polrock* collared with black fur survives in the Landesmuseum, and bears the Prussian Order of the Red Eagle: whether the duke would have worn the star of the order in action is unknown. He would almost certainly have worn the officer's sash, as being the only clearly visible sign of rank on this plain outfit. The belt, hangers and sabre are preserved in the Landesmuseum. Schröder and Ackermann both show tight hussar breeches tucked into plain-looking hessian boots; the Jones sketch, and the Hourtelle plate (followed by C. A. Norman in his *Tradition* article) both show striped, reinforced overalls worn over the boots; since we have gone this far with Schröder, we have picked the former, more or less by guesswork. (The pipe, however, is well attested: we have eyewitness accounts of the Black Duke strolling back and forth, smoking in a leisurely manner, in an attempt to calm his nervous troops by example.)

G3: Sergeant-major, Leib-Bataillon (see pp. 39–40)

Based to some extent on Beyer-Pegau for standard distinctions of this rank (including the cane, now carried by sergeants and upward), this figure also illustrates a most interesting infantry dolman or 'Spencer' now displayed in the Landesmuseum. The silver crown and chevrons and the facing of the Leib-Bataillon are conventional: but the black chest

(*Left*)
Officer of Horse Artillery, 1815. The shako has a black velvet top band, a silver death's-head plate, a gold grenade below this, and gilt chin scales with lion-mask bosses. The uniform is black faced with black, with gold lace embroidery at collar and cuffs, and gold trouser stripes. The pouch belt is shown as gold lace, with gilt picker equipment; the sash and sabre knot are conventional silver and yellow.

(*Centre*)
Surviving shako, identified as that of an officer of Horse Artillery, 1815. The top is black leather, the top and bottom bands are both black velvet, the death's-head is silver and the grenade gilt. Note the chin scale boss, with a silver running horse badge on a gilt rosette. The shako—today, at least—has a very exaggerated taper, appearing almost bell-shaped from the side. (Landesmuseum Braunschweig)

(*Right*)
Driver, Train of Foot Artillery, 1815. The dark brownish-grey drab uniform is faced black and piped yellow, with black leather reinforcement to the overalls and black leather equipment. Yellow pompon on shako, brass grenade badge on pouch.

lacing is as shown—of fine officer quality, and ending in two trefoils at the front of the shoulders, which show no sign of ever having borne shoulder straps. There is black-on-black lace decoration above the cuffs; and the collar is edged with black braid.

H1: Private, 2nd Line Battalion (see p. 40)
H2: Company officer, 1st Line Battalion, with Herzogs-fahne (see pp. 40, 43)
H3: Drummer, 1st Line Battalion (see p. 41)

Notes sur les planches en couleur

A1 Shako en feutre et cuir de fabrication autrichienne, ne différant du type porté par l'infanterie que par ses écailles de mentonnière en laiton. Parement de manchettes blue pâle cousu à l'extérieur des manches seulement. Trompette distingué par l'habituel 'nid d'hirondelle' or et noir. La cartouchière portait un insigne de tête de mort en argent. **A2** Shako et paletot *Litewka*, comme officiers d'infanterie; ceinture en tissu argent et jaune; insigne à tête de mort sur sabretache. **A3** Liséré rouge sur l'arrière du corps de *kurtka* et coutures de manche; cartouchière et sabre de type hussar.

B1 *Litewka* avec fente unique à l'arrière; les sources diffèrent sur la couleur des manchettes mais noir est considéré plus probable que bleu pâle. Equipement en cuir autrichien; cartouchière simple. Sous-officiers (probablement) distingués par différents noeuds de l'épée; ils portaient des sabres ainsi que des bayonnettes mais pas de canes à cette date. **B2** Certaines sources mais pas toutes montrent des écailles de mentonnière en argent. Noter les olivets supplémentaires sur les passements de poitrine de *Litewka*; sabre de cavalerie légère en acier et fourreau noir avec noeud d'épée argent et noir. **B3** Noter le plumet en plumes de coq *Jäger* spécial; long paletot à aiguillettes; ceinture et sabre comme officier d'infanterie. **B4** Les revers de la veste étaient rouges; les pantalons soit blancs soit gris. Noter le rebord du chapeau effectivement retournés du gauche et non droit. Sac à bandouillère en cuir noir—*Ranzentasche*—et bayonnette *Hirschfänger* sur la hanche gauche.

C1 Les seules différences depuis 1809 étaient la ceinture en tissu bleu clair et rouge; la ceinture à cartouches sans taquets à chainette; pantalons plutôt que salopette, nouvelle pelisse; et, pour les sous-officiers, chevrons de style britannique en blanc ou argent. **C2** Noter la bande or de shako et le nouveau *dolman*, faisant ressembler les officiers aux hommes de troupe davantage qu'en 1809. Ceinture en tissu or et rouge et noeud d'été de style britannique.

D1 Noter la nouvelle veste courte ressemblant au *dolman*. L'équipement personnel et les armes—et les insignes de sous-officiers—étaient maintenant de type britannique; havresac comme D3. **D2** Là aussi, noter la nouvelle veste *dolman*; ceinture en tissu d'infanterie légère britannique et noeud d'épée. **D3** Shako comme pour l'infanterie; veste boutonnée sur le devant avec col, manchettes, revers bleu pâle; équipement comme pour l'infanterie sauf pour bayonnette et fusil *Baker* de fabrication britannique.

E1 Uniforme à parements dans les couleurs du bataillon; les grades au-dessus de major avaient des noeuds noirs et non argent au-dessus des manchettes. En service, les majors et grades au-dessus portaient une cartouchière noire et une ceinture noire, le revers de la cartouchière avait un monogramme '*FW*' argent. **E2** Bleu pâle était maintenant la couleur des parements du *Leib-Btl.* seulement. Noter que la ceinture en tissu et le noeud de sabre étaient maintenant de nouveau argent et jaune. **E3** Comparer avec H3, tambour ordinaire, pour voir les différences des détails de l'uniforme.

F1 Là aussi, noter le rebord de chapeau retourné du côté gauche—et voir photo d'accompagnement. **F2** Le chapeau, avec un insigne de clairon au lieu du cheval caracolant des Jägers était la seule chose qui distinguait ces troupes de l'infanterie ordinaire; ils portaient des parements verts et étaient équipés de mousquets. **F3** Noter l'insigne de shako spécial des bataillons légers; les couleurs de parement étaient chamois (1er), jaune (2ème) et orange (3ème). Noter aussi les distinctions de sous-officiers—sabre; chevrons de grade britanniques; cartouchière sur l'estomac et non sur l'épaule et, pour les sergents, ceinture en tissu et gants blancs. Ces caractéristiques étaient communes aux sous-officiers de toutes les unités d'infanterie. **F4** Seul l'insigne de shako et la couleur de parement de bataillon distinguent les simples soldats de l'infanterie légère de l'infanterie de ligne.

G1 Coupe et style d'uniforme comme en 1809, mais maintenant dans des couleurs nouvelles. **G2** Cette reconstitution est, franchement, de la devinette, empruntant des caractéristiques de plusieurs portraits différents, tous posthumes. Le képi est essentiellement la coiffe de petite tenue des officiers Hussars avec des passements argent supplémentaire en forme de feuilles. Noter qu'un gland argent pouvait retomber du rondeau en passement au centre de la couronne. Le *Polrock* garni de fourrure et le sabre sont dans le *Landesmuseum* de Brunswick. **G3** Basé partiellement sur Beyer-Pegau et partiellement sur une intéressante veste '*Spencer*' dans le *Landesmuseum*—noter le mélange de caractéristiques d'officier et de sous-officier dans la décoration et les passements.

H1 Tous les bataillons portaient cet insigne de shako et des uniformes identiques sauf pour les couleurs de parement: rouge (1er), vert (2ème) et blanc (3ème). **H2** A part les parements de couleur et les détails du shako, comme E2. Les officiers des bataillons légers portaient des gants verts, ceux des bataillons de ligne, des gants blancs. **H3** L'emploi du shako *Kiwer* de style russe n'était pas spécial aux tambours ou à une unité particulière—plusieurs semblent avoir été portés par les hommes de troupe, comme élément de distribution aléatoire.

Farbtafeln

A1 In österreich hergestellter Tschako aus Filz und Leder, der sich von der Infanterie-Version Lediglich durch seine Kinnband-Halterungen aus Messing unterschied. Lediglich an den Aussenseiten der Ärmel war ein hellblauer Manschettenbesatz angenäht. Der Trompeter wurde durch ein übliches 'Schwalbennest' hervorgehoben. Die Tasche truge eine silberne Totenkopf-Spange. **A2** Tschako und *Litewka*-Mantel der Infanterieoffiziere; Schärpe in Silber und Gelb; Totenkopf-Spange auf der *sabretasche*. **A3** Rote Paspeln am Rücken der Körperund Ärmelnähte der *kurtka*; Tasche und Säbel wie die Husaren.

B1 *Litewka* mit einem hinteren Schlitz; es gibt verschiedene Berichte über die Manschettenfarbe, Schwarz ist aber insgesamt eher wahrscheinlich als Hellblau österreichische Lederausstattung; einfache Tasche. unteroffiziere hoben sich (vermutlich) durch andere Schwertknoten ab: sie trugen neben Säbeln auch Bajonette aber zu dieser Zeit noch keine Stöcke. **B2** Einige, jedoch nicht alle Quellen zeigen silberne Kinnband-Halterungen. Auffällig sind die zusätzlichen Knebel an der Brusttresse der *Litewka*; leichter Kavalleriesäbel aus blankem Stahl mit Schwarz, mit silbernem und gelbem Schwertknoten. **B3** Auffällig ist die spezielle Hahnen-Schmuckfeder der *Jäger*; langer Gehrock mit *aiguillettes*; Gürtel und Säbel wie beim Infanterieoffizier. **B4** Die Jackenaufschläge waren rot; die Hosen entweder weiss oder grau. Auffällig ist die Hutkrempe, die statt rechts auf der linken Seite hochgeschlagen ist. Schwarze Leder-Ranzentasche—und *Hirschfänger*-Bajonett an der linken Hüfte.

C1 Die einzigen Unterschiede seit 1809 bestanden in einer hellblauen und roter Schärpe; Taschengürtel ohne Stechnadeln; Reithosen anstelle der Overalls; neue *pelisse*; und bei den Unteroffizieren weisse oder silberne Winkel im britischen Stil. **C2** Auffällig ist das goldene Tschako-Band; und durch den neuen *Dolman* sahen die Offiziere mehr wie Soldaten aus als 1809. Goldene und rote Schärpe sowie Schwertknoten im britischen Stil.

D1 Auffällig ist die neue, kurze Jacke wie ein *Dolman*. Die persönliche Ausstattung und die Waffen—einschliesslich der Unteroffiziers-Rangabzeichen—waren in britischer Art gehalten. Tornister wie D3. **D2** Wiederum auffällig ist die blaue Dolman-Jacke; britische Schärpe der leichten Infanterie und Schwertknoten. **D3** Tschako wie für die Infanterie; einreihige Jacke mit hellblauen Kragen, Manschetten und Aufschlägen; abgesehen von dem britischen *Baker*-Gewehr und dem Bajonett Ausstattung wie für die Infanterie.

E1 Uniform mit Besatz in den Bataillonsfarben; die Dienstgrade unterhalb des Majors hatten statt der silbernen schwarze Knöpfe oberhalb der Manschetten. Im Dienst trugen die Dienstgrade ab Major aufwärts eine schwarze Tasche mit Gürtel, wobei die Taschenklappe ein silberne *FW*-Ziffer trug. **E2** Hellblau war nun ausschliesslich die Besatzfarbe des *Leib-Btl.* Auffällig ist, dass Schärpe und Säbelknoten wieder silber und gelb geworden sind. **E3** Zum Vergleich der Uniformdetails mit H3: ein einfacher Trommler.

F1 Wiederum auffällig ist, dass die Krempe links hochgeschlagen ist—beachten Sie auch das dazugehörige Foto. **F2** Der Hut, der eine Jagdhorn-Spange anstelle des springenden Pferdes der Jäger trug, war der einzige Unterschied dieser Soldaten gegenüber der normalen Infanterie: sie hatten grüne Besatz und trugen Musketen. **F3** Auffällig ist die spezielle Tschako-Spange des Leichten Bataillons: die Besatzfarben waren braungelb (1.), gelb (2.) und orange (3.) Auffällig sind auch die Unterschiedsmerkmale der Unteroffiziere—Säbel; britische Winkel-Rangabzeichen; Tasche am Bauch statt über der Schulter und für Feldwebel Schärpen und weisse Handschuhe. Diese Merkmale waren den Unteroffizieren aller Infanterieeinheiten gemeinsam. **F4** Nur die Tschako-Spange und die Bataillons-Besatzfarbe unterschied die Gefreiten der Leichten von denen der regulären Infanterie.

G1 Schnitt und Stil der Uniform wie im Jahre 1809, jetzt aber in neuen Farben. **G2** Ehrlich gesagt, beruht diese Rekonstruktion nur auf Vermutungen, wobei nachträglich die Merkmale von verschiedenen Portraits zusammengesetzt wurden. Die Mütze ist im Grunde die Dienst-Kopfbedeckung der Husarenoffiziere, mit zusätzlichen, blattförmigem Silberband; Auffällig ist auch, dass eventuell in der Mitte einer Textilkokarde mitten in der Krone Silberquaste herabhing. Der *Polrock* mit Pelzbesatz befindet sich, ebenso wie der Säbel, im Braunschweiger *Landesmuseum*. **G3** Dies beruht teils auf Beyer-Pegau und teils auf einer interessanten *Spencer*-Jacke im *Landesmuseum*—auffällig ist die Mischung von Unteroffiziers- und Offiziersmerkmalen bei der Dekoration und bei der Tresse.

H1 Alle Bataillone trugen diese Tschako-Spange und, bis auf die Besatzfarben identischen Uniformen: rot (1.), grün (2.) un weiss (3.) **H2** Abgesehen von der farbigen Besätzen und den Tschako-Details waren diese die gleichen wie E2. Die Offiziere der leichten Bataillone trugen grüne, die der regulären Bataillone weisse Handschuhe. **H3** Die Verwendung der *Kiwer*-Tschakos im russischen Stil war nicht allein den Trommlern oder bestimmten Einheiten vorbehalten—eine Reihe dieser Tschakos wurde willkürlich von allen Rängen getragen.